Copyright © 2005 Omnibus Press
A Division of *The* **Music Sales** *Group*

Written by Lou G. Stone
Picture research, cover, and book design by Sarah Nesenjuk

ISBN 0.8256.3437.7
Order NO. OP51238

All rights reserved. No part of this book may be reproduced in any form or by any electronic or mechanical means, including information stoage or retrieval systems, without permimssion in writing from the publisher, except by a reviewer who may quote brief passages.

Exclusive Distributors:
Music Sales Corporation
257 Park Avenue South, New York, NY 10010, U.S.A.
Music Sales Limited
8/9 Frith Street, London W1D 3JB, U.K.
Music Sales Pty. Limited
120 Rothschild Street, Rosbery, Sydney, NSW 2018, Australia

Photo Credits:
Front cover: Kevin Estrada/Retna
Back cover: Frank White
Carlo Allegri/Getty Images: page 59
Michel Boutefeu/Getty Images: pages 12, 23, 44 and 75
Scott Gries/Getty Images: pages 18L, 32 and 42
Scott Harrison/Getty Images: pages 1, 51 and 54
Ian Jennings/Scope/LFI: pages 52-53
Jen Lowery/LFI: page 90
Soren McCarty/WireImage: pages 3, 14-15, 31, 38-39, 68, 73, 76, 80, 82, 85 and 94-95
David Ray/LFI: page 6
Frank White: pages 4-5, 8, 11, 16, 18R, 19-21, 24, 28, 34, 36T, 36B, 40, 41T, 41B, 48-50, 51B, 55T, 55B, 56, 60, 64, 66-67, 70-71, 74, 78-79, 86, 88, 89L, 89R, 92-93 and 96
Photo of fire featured on front cover and throughout interior: Ben Lawry/Retna

Printed in the United States of America
Visit Omnibus Press at www.omnibuspress.com

OMNIBUS PRESS PRESENTS THE STORY OF

Insane Clown Posse

By Lou G. Stone

OMNIBUS PRESS
LONDON · NEW YORK · SYDNEY

Introduction ...7
Life At Risk ...9
I'm Not Alone ...13
F**k Off! ...17
The Dark Carnival Is Coming To Town ...25
Carnival Of Carnage ...29
The Ringmaster ...35
Hellalujah ...45
On The Road And In The Ring ...61
WWF ...65
Jack And Jake ...69
The Bomb ...77
Juggalo Nation ...81
Thy Unveiling ...87
Like It Like That ...91
Discography ...93

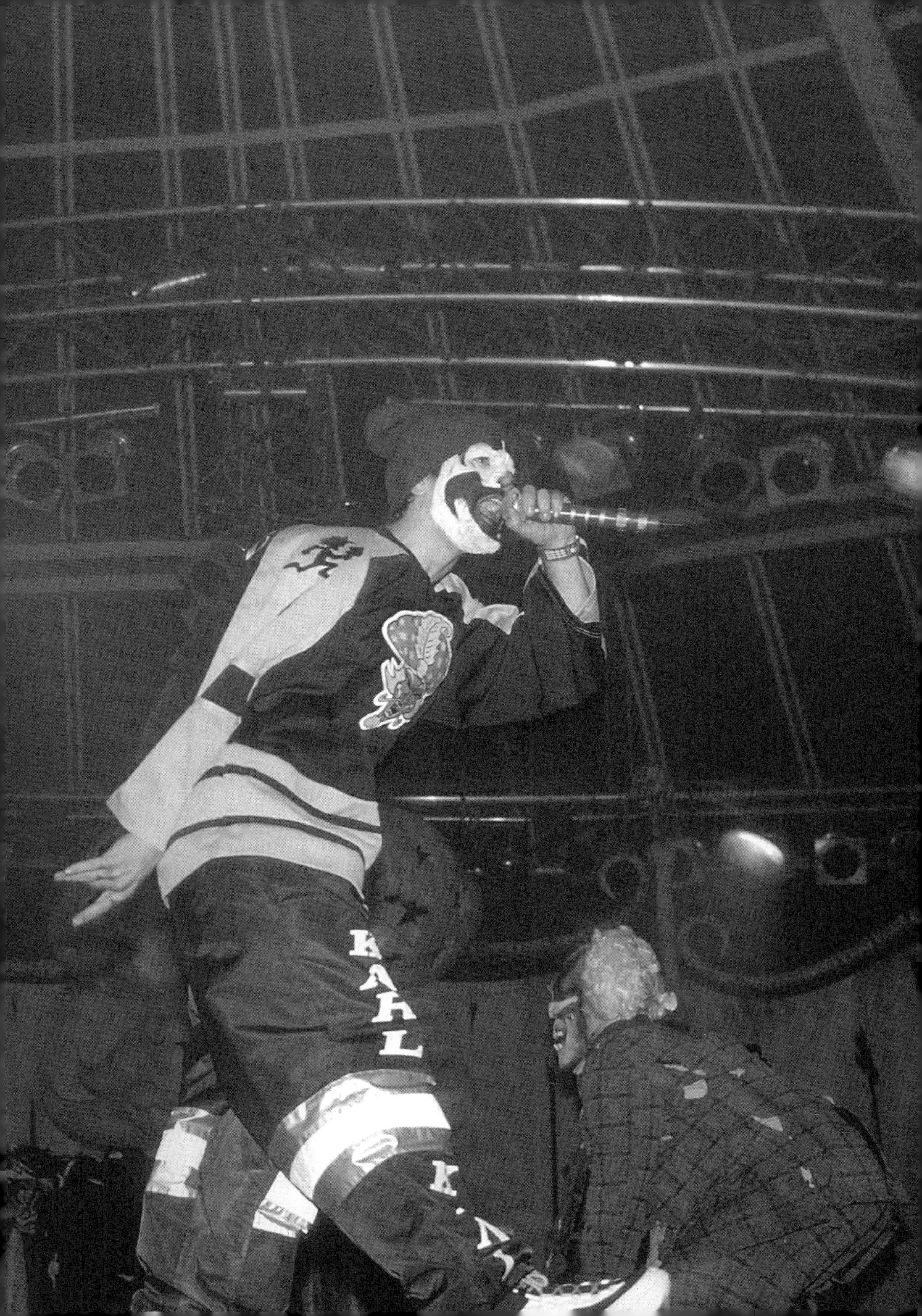

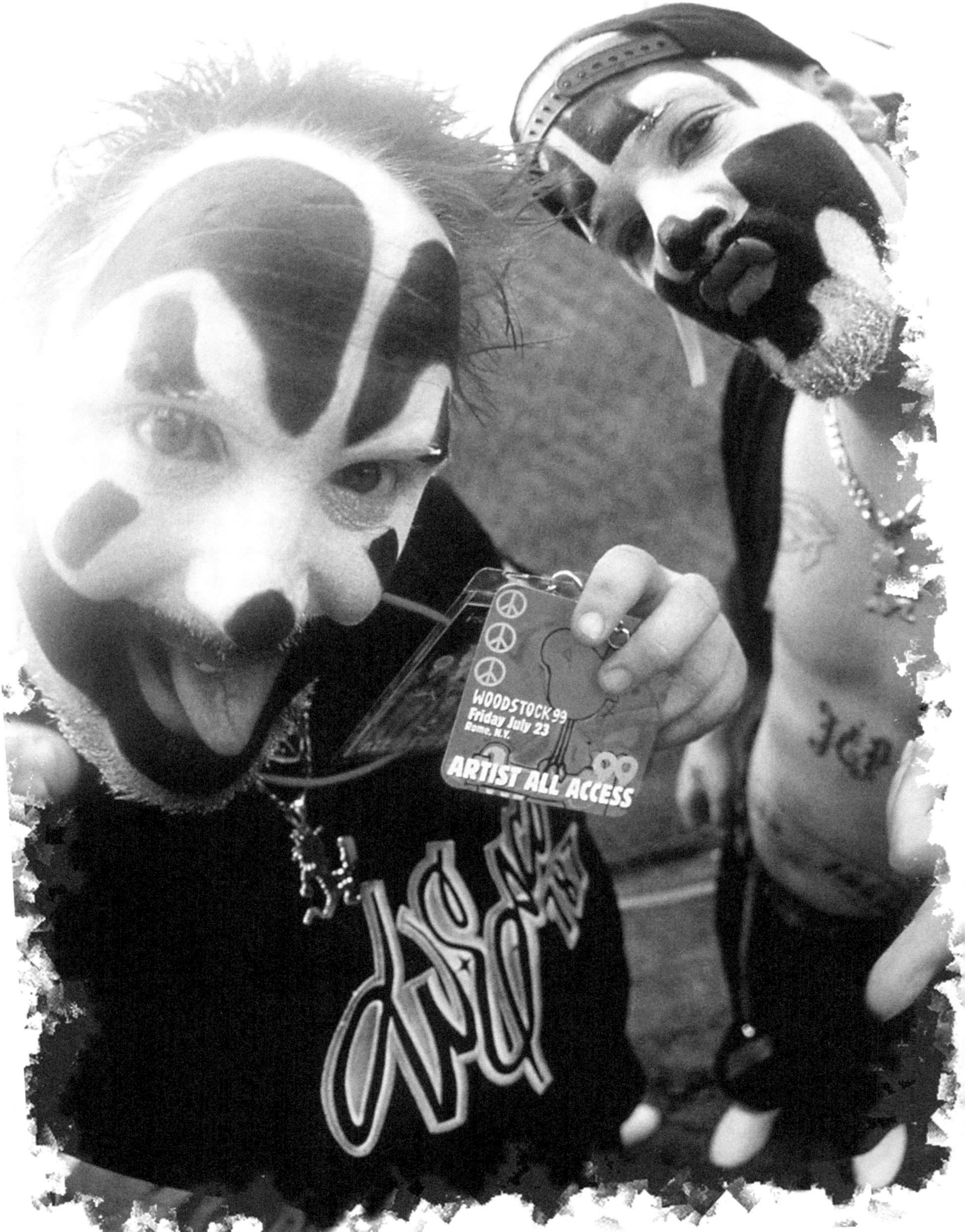
WOODSTOCK 99
Friday July 23
Rome, N.Y.
ARTIST ALL ACCESS

Introduction

In 1991, rap ruled Detroit. From the depths of its thriving local music scene emerged a crew like none other: The Insane Clown Posse. With their greasepaint-covered visages and graphic, horror-laden lyrics, they staked a claim in the history of extreme and outrageous Detroit rockers, somewhere between the polarities of rap and metal. Reviled and misunderstood by just about everyone who's heard of them, and shunned by the music-industry machine, ICP nevertheless built a loyal following of Juggalos and eventually, a music empire.

Violent J. (Joe Bruce) and Shaggy 2 Dope (Joey Utsler) are seemingly society's worst nightmare. The overwhelming majority of their songs have to be labeled "explicit." Their lyrics are vile, misogynistic, obscene, and violent, not to mention juvenile. They've adopted the personas of evil, serial killing, gangsta clowns who transmit messages from a mysterious supernatural entity known as the Dark Carnival.

They've got no regard for other people's property, or their own, for that matter. They throw bottles at and copiously spray their fans with Faygo, a low-budget brand of "pop." Like other Midwesterners, they call soda pop.

Characters aside, they're reknown for their stupid behavior. They attack fans with mics, get into brawls in diners, beat up D.J.'s, exchange insults with Sharon Osbourne, and generally bite any music-industry hand that contemplates feeding them (okay, these last two admittedly aren't so bad).

They're into wrestling.

After writing this book, I want to hop a plane to Detroit and smack them on their respective noses with a rolled up newspaper because they deserve it. I'd do it too, except they'd enjoy it too much, f**king bastards.

That said, there's something extremely appealing about them. They've remained outsiders in an insider's world. They're floobs, scrubs, and losers—just like us.

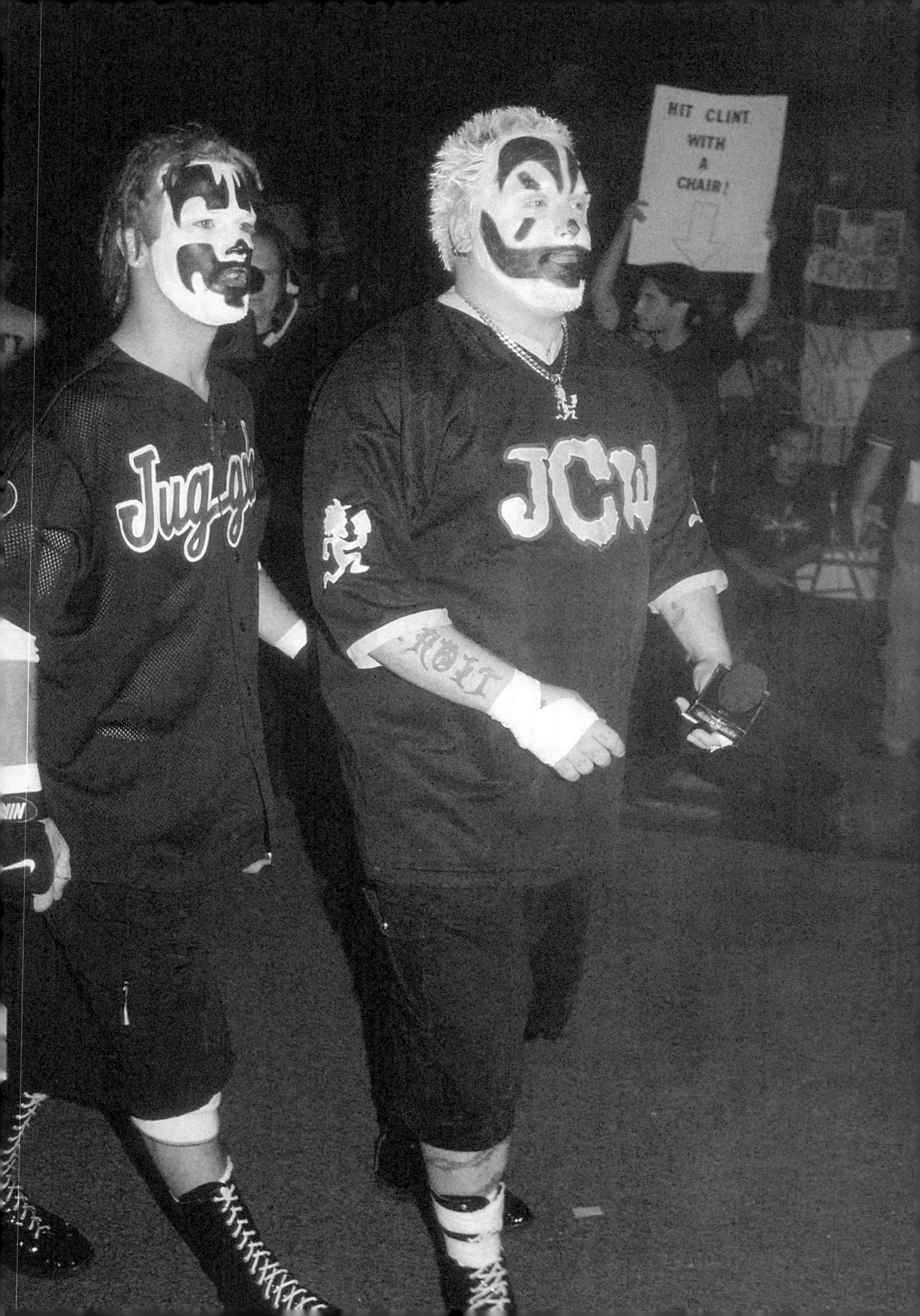
HIT CLINT
WITH
A
CHAIR!
JCW

Life At Risk

Detroit, Michigan: The name once conjured images of factory lines and industry, an urban center whose most notable product, the automobile, represented the vision and ingenuity of America, as well as its promise of safety and prosperity in exchange for hard work. But in the late Sixties and early Seventies, as the United States as a whole began to confront the aftermath of centuries of racial repression and the robust post-World War II industrial economy began to slow, Detroit came to represent the explosion of racial tensions, as well as urban decay and neglect. Life in Detroit's projects was filled with violence and economic despair.

Joseph Bruce (aka Violent J.) was born on April 28, 1972 and his early life was spent in Berkley, a suburb located three miles north of Detroit. Although you might think that a suburban childhood would be a dream in comparison to coming up in the rough streets of the city itself, for Joe it was no cakewalk.

After a rocky relationship, Joe's parents Rick and Linda Bruce, split up when he was two. His father disappeared from the picture altogether, and Linda struggled to raise Joe and his two older siblings, Theresa and Rob, on her own. She worked long hours and still had to depend on donations to feed and clothe the family. Despite the fact that they were poor, Joe remembers his early childhood as a relatively happy time. "At the elementary school level of life...you don't really give a f**k if you're poor," Joe recalls in the band's autobiography penned with *Detroit Free Press* music writer Hobey Echlin, *ICP: Behind the Paint*. "Nobody does...All you really care about is playing, adventure, pretending,

The Story of I.C.P.

and all that fresh-ass little kid shit that comes for free in life."

Poverty wasn't the only obstacle that the Bruce's would encounter. His mother's second marriage, when Joe was six years old, turned out to be a disaster for the struggling family. The marriage lasted two years, during which time Joe and his older siblings endured bizarre and abusive behavior from their stepfather. His mother worked multiple jobs to support the family and was frequently out of the house. Linda kicked him out as soon as she found out about his behavior, but the family was profoundly affected. Her relationship with Theresa, who was the oldest, was tumultuous for years afterward.

Between their mother's heavy work schedule and her pre-occupation with their sister's self-destructive behavior, Joe and his older brother Rob were often on their own. They spent copious amounts of time running around their neighborhood—exploring nearby forests was a favorite pastime. While Rob delved further and further into role-playing games such as Dungeons and Dragons and other fantasy games, Joe loved ninja movies and pro-wrestling. Their self-reliance, active imaginations, and close relationship got them through many a tough time.

Those active imaginations may be at the heart of some of the otherworldly experiences Joe and Rob recount from their youth, experiences which Joe believes eventually led to his visions of the Dark Carnival, the mythology on which the Insane Clown Posse is based. When Joe was five years old, he describes a dark, black "oil" figure visiting him and his brother when a neighborhood bully slept over at their house. That figure, they believed, was God visiting them to let them know everything would be all right.

One of the brothers' favorite places to explore was an undeveloped stretch of land near their home, which they dubbed Picker Forest. In *Behind the Paint*, Joe describes it as a creepy place, filled with ghosts and spirits. One time, he and his brother walked by an abandoned house, and Joe threw a golf ball into one of the broken-out basement windows. "All of a sudden, it came back up to the window and stayed there, right in the middle of the window, right in mid-air, floating in the darkness...We were so scared, we ran like motherf**kers...and we never, ever found that house again."

Another time, he describes a friend freaking out during his first (and only) trek through the forest. According to Joe, the friend swore he'd been there in another life, and proved it by describing and then leading them to a yellow fire hydrant on a dead-end road, which led to nowhere. As loopy as these stories sound, Joe still swears they, and other similar encounters he had later in life, are true.

Eventually his mother remarried once again, and the family moved from Berkley to the rougher neighborhood of Oak Park, which was located several miles closer to Detroit. At the time, Joe and his brother had the typical issues with their new stepfather as any kids might, but in retrospect, Joe gives him his props. "By the time Ron came into our lives, to be honest, I think I was just finished with the

Life At Risk

whole dad thing anyway," he recounts in *ICP: Behind the Paint*. "I pretty much ignored all of his household laws. Nowadays, I respect and love him for staying with my mom, and helping us out so much all them years. He was by far the best dad I ever had."

While their life at home began to improve, the older the Bruce brothers got, the tougher school life became. As early as middle school, other kids started to make fun of their outward trappings of poverty. From late payments on school lunches to hand-me-down clothes and bikes, it was all fodder for their schoolmates. The more that other kids treated them as outcasts, however, the more Joe and Rob began to embrace their underdog status. They dubbed themselves and what few friends they had "the Floobs."

"Before there were Juggalos, you see, there were Floobs," explains Joe in *Behind the Paint*. "We wore the same old shoes and shitty clothes from rummage sales, but to us, we didn't have to be cool, because we were Floobs! Everybody else had dope-ass bikes—you remember Mongooses and Supergooses? Well, we never had no shit like that. If you had a beat-up Huffy with a banana seat and a steering wheel for handlebars, then you had a Floobmobile. We turned our scrubbiness into something we could be proud of."

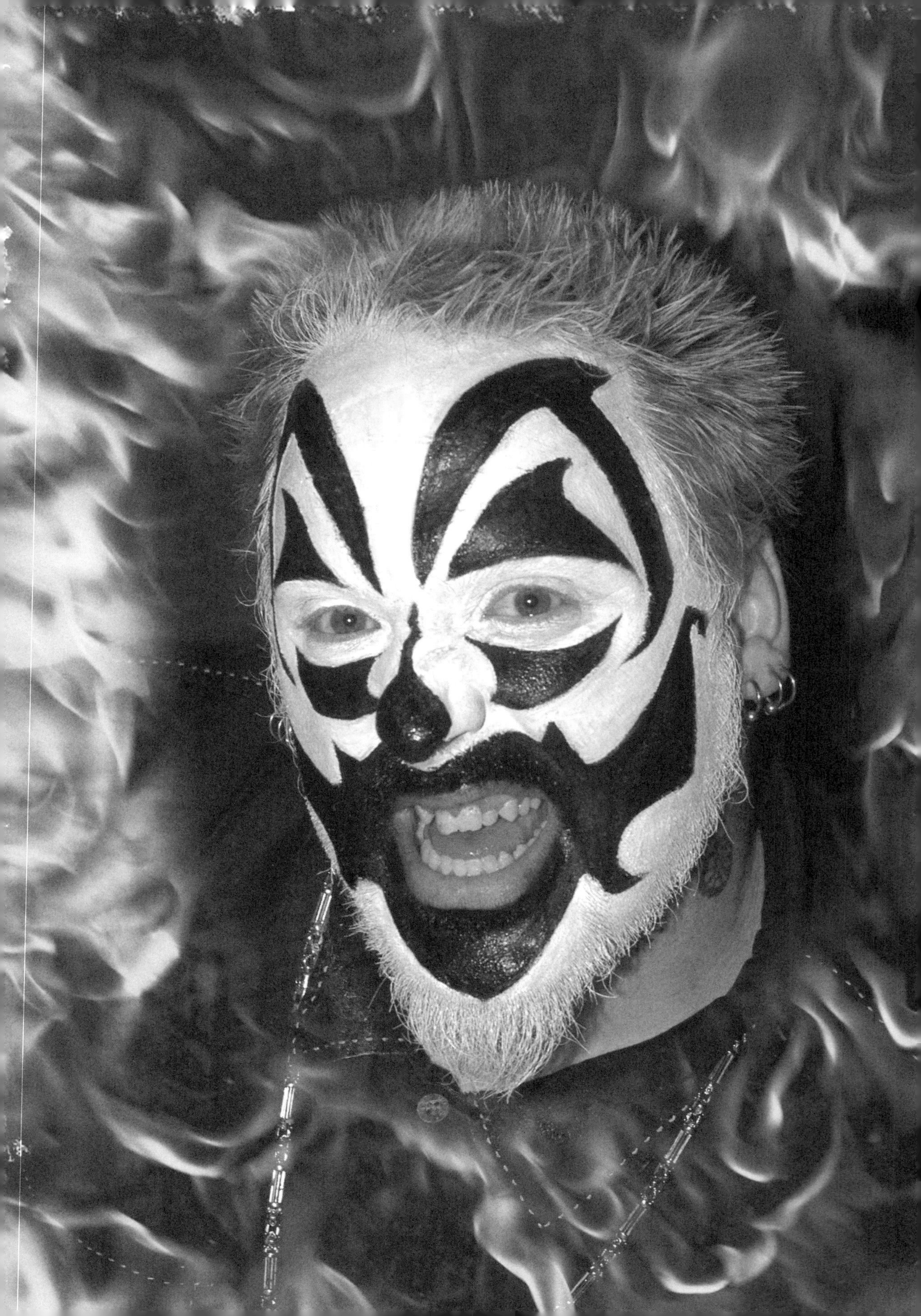

I'm Not Alone

The family's move to Oak Park brought Joe and Rob closer to Detroit and in closer contact with a much tougher, more streetwise student body at Best Junior High School. Both brothers learned to stand up for themselves—striking back hard against anyone who messed with them. This, of course, became easier once they gained some friends. The first friend Joe made after he started 7th Grade, was John Utsler, who had also recently moved to the school from the same neighborhood as Joe and Rob. Joe's friendship with John and his younger brother Joey (who would later become Shaggy 2 Dope) would be a long-lasting one, cemented first by a shared fascination with wrestling and later, rap music.

The friends started their own backyard wrestling federation—Tag Team Wrestling (TTW)—building an outside ring at Joey and John's mother's house in nearby Ferndale, as well as one in their friend Lacy's backyard in Royal Oak Township, an even poorer and more dangerous neighborhood than Oak Park, comparable, according to Joe, to L.A.'s notorious Compton area. Their wrestling forays to the Township were Joe's first introduction to a truly impoverished neighborhood. Despite the fact that most of the Township kids rejected him because he was white, he felt an affinity for them.

"Hanging out with Lacy in the Township was my first experience with a bad neighborhood," Joe relates in *Behind the Paint*. "...As new as all this was to me, it was also kind of familiar. The Township kids were on welfare, and got food from the hunger barrel; it felt like a whole neighborhood of Bruce Brothers." Joe never knew how he'd be treated when he visited the Township. "Some days I'm having fun," he recalls. "Other days I'm getting shot at, and somebody else is having the fun."

The Story of I.C.P.

Around the same time, Joe, John, and Joey were also getting into rap: Run DMC, UTFO, the Geto Boys, the Beastie Boys, and NWA were just a few of the bands they were into. They weren't just listening to the music. They began to dress the part, with Kangol tracksuits, just about anything Adidas they could lay their hands on, and when the Beastie Boys' Mike D. started wearing a VW medallion, they followed suit. Joey in particular was adept at swiping hood ornaments. When Graffiti became big, they tagged too, as the Krylon Boys.

Not long thereafter, they recorded their first track under the crew name, the JJ Boys. The song, "Party at the Top of the Hill," was recorded on a friend's four-track tape recorder. "We're the JJ Boys on the microphone stand / Kickin' it live with a Faygo in our hand / Master T is on the table, not working in the stable / And on his Adidas jacket is the Faygo label" Even in the group's infancy, Joe and Joey are sharing the love for Faygo pop, which now figures so prominently in ICP lore.

Faygo, for the uninitiated, is the budget pop of Detroit. In addition to the allure of a cheap price tag, Faygo offers a dizzying array of flavors, of which Moon Mist, Redpop, and Rock & Rye are the most inventively named. Despite the group's inclusion of their products in lyrics and performances over the past fourteen or so years, Faygo hasn't embraced Insane Clown Posse or its fans with the same level of enthusiam.

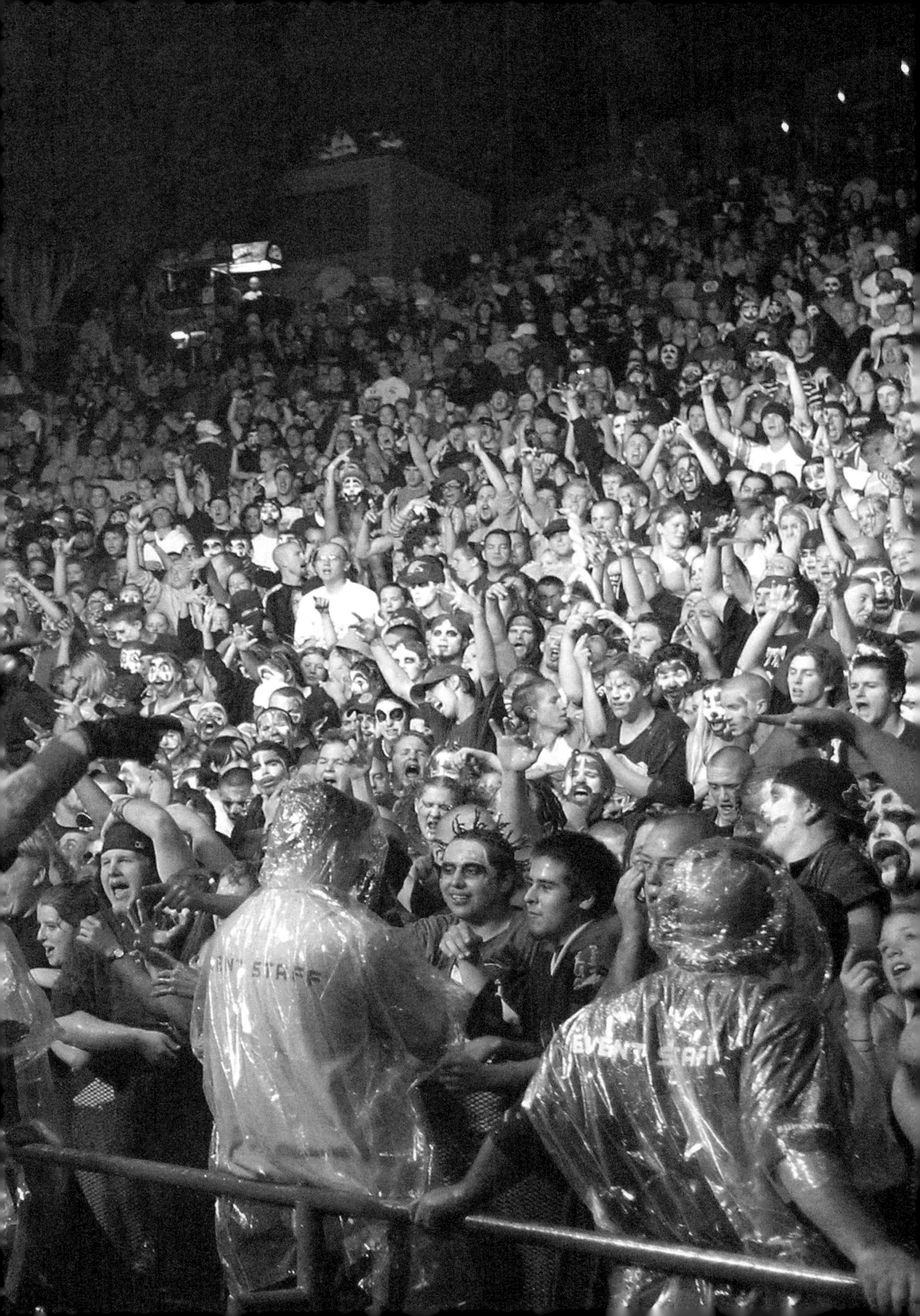

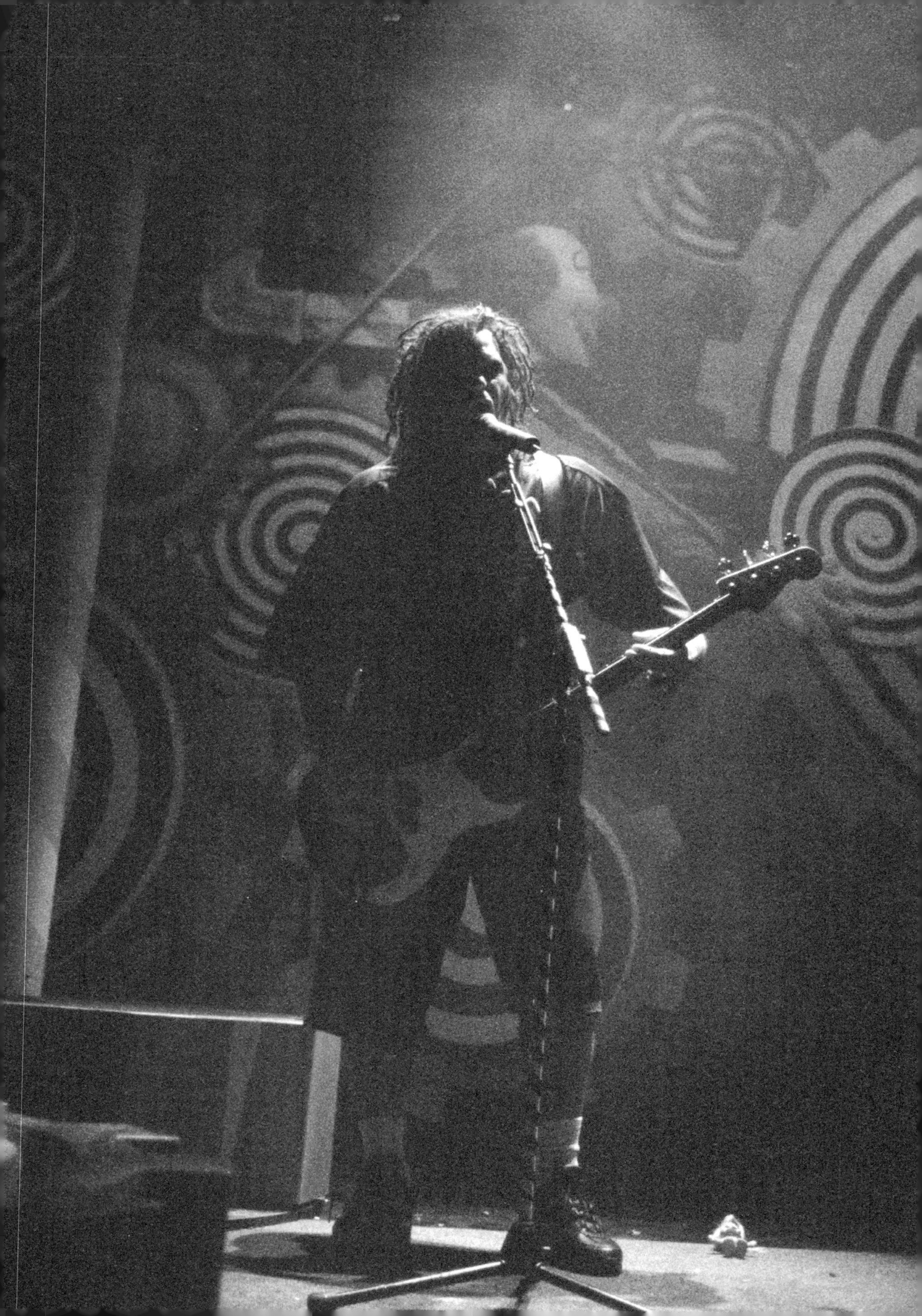

F**k Off!

While Joe's fascination with wrestling and rap music was growing, his interest in school was waning. Hardly surprising, given the fact that, aside from a few inept attempts by Best Junior High's principal to scare him into bringing up his grades, his teachers left him to his own devices. When he made it to class, he was late; class time was spent either sleeping or drawing; and assignments, well...what was the point? Things came to a head in his freshman year of high school. After a confrontation with a teacher one afternoon—he'd been dropping encyclopedias out the window—Joe walked out for good. It wasn't unexpected; both Theresa and Rob dropped out before they graduated from high school.

Rob headed into the military. Without his older brother around to keep him positive, years being treated like an outsider caught up with Joe as he approached his mid-teens. Although he was still into wrestling—he and Joey would sneak into World Wrestling Federation and WCW shows whenever they came through downtown Detroit's Joe Louis and Cobo Arenas—his major preoccupation was the gang they formed—the Inner City Posse. In addition to friends from Ferndale, the gang included Lacy and other guys from the Township, as well as fellow wrestling fan Rudy "Rude Boy" who lived in Downriver, another rough neighborhood in Southwest Detroit.

"With my mom having so much trouble raising my sister, Rob and I basically raised each other," Joe recalls in *Behind the Paint*. "Only now Rob was gone. He was always my anchor, without him I was lost...For the first time, I was pissed about the bad breaks my family always got...I fell off hard, with no net. I was mad at everything. I never got into drugs, but that's just because my friends weren't into them. I was lost enough to try anything. I didn't care enough not to do drugs. I had no choice but to trade my brother, and all of our special Bruce Brother honor, in for a stale life of trying to be a badass. I was trying to catch up for all the years of blowing it all off."

Joe concedes that in comparison to what other kids were doing, Inner City Posse wasn't a true gang. "Real gangs sold drugs or guns; we were just terrorizing people." Real gang or no, they quickly became adept at doling out their share of random violence and over time managed to build up solid résumés of petty crime. They may not have considered themselves authentic gang bangers, but their victims probably couldn't see the distinction. "All we did was beat up rich people, or anybody with a mouth," says Joe. "Sometimes the fights were with other crews

F**K Off!

who thought they were hard. We would rush them with all the weapons in my car, and leave them broken and bloody." Enmities developed during this period would follow ICP down the road.

Joe's anger was coming out in all facets of his life. Missy, a girl he'd been dating who lived in the wealthy suburb of Milford, stopped seeing him. He beat up the kid she'd started dating—at a school dance at her high school, on the dance floor in front of students and teachers. After that incident he started calling her and threatening her. His behavior would soon come back to haunt him.

Eventually, gang life caught up with the crew. Joe, John, and Joey were arrested for trying to steal a car stereo. John and Joey were released immediately, but unfortunately for Joe, there was a warrant out for his arrest for the threatening phone calls he'd been making to Missy. Joe languished in the Oakland County bullpen for a week—no one had the $100 to post bond. Despite the rough week he spent in lock up—a fellow inmate beat him up after he refused to hand over his jacket, his belligerent behavior in front of the judge landed him right back in lock up for another two weeks. Once again, no one had money to post bail, and this time he graduated to being held in "the real" jail. A slow learner, he was once again beat up, this time for inadvertently suggesting that a fellow cellmate had stolen his breakfast.

After two weeks, Joe got out on probation, with a restraining order that banned him from the city of Milford. Instead of laying low, Joe immediately went to find Missy, and landed back in Oakland County Jail, this time for ninety days. He spent Christmas and New Year's Day in jail: His only visitors were Joey and his mother. Joe spent most of his sentence writing raps to pass the time.

The Story of I.C.P.

He was seventeen years old, a high-school dropout with a record; it was time for a change.

When he got out, he hooked up with Rudy, who at this point was working for a promoter for a local independent wrestling league. The pair talked their way into the ring—Joe wrestled his first match as Corporal Darryl Daniels in Army gear his brother had sent him. Joe's stint on the local indie wrestling circuit was an eye opener. Needless to say, professional wrestling didn't live up to Joe's childhood fantasies and—more to the point—he wasn't making any money. He quickly came to the conclusion that the wrestling scene wasn't his bag.

F**K Off!

Aside from wrestling and working menial jobs to stay afloat and out of trouble, Joe began spending more time working out raps. In *Behind the Paint*, he describes recording his first album, *Enter the Ghetto Zone*. "I took two tape players and turned them to face each other," he recalls. "I hit record on one, and play on the other. As the one tape player played the beat [Joe used cassette recordings of any instrumental versions of raps he could find], I stuck my head in-between both radios and rapped. The recording tape player caught both the beat coming out of the other radio and my voice rapping." He rapped as Violent J., which was his street name in the Inner City Posse gang.

The Story of I.C.P.

Joe recorded the next album *Ghetto Territory* with John and Joey as Inner City Posse, using the same method. They followed up with a second album soon there after, in 1991. ICP produced *Bassment Cuts* on a karaoke (bought, along with blank cassettes, by Violent J.'s then-girlfriend, Karen). The crew fell back on some "creative" strategies (shoplifting and pawning stolen car stereos) to finance the purchase of back-up instrumentals.

With his experience promoting for indie wrestling, Rudy was doing a brisk volume of sales with *Bassment Cuts* in Southwest. ICP was attracting attention, but not all of it was welcome. In that murky mix of rap crews and gangs, much of it was coming from old enemies and rival crews who knew that ICP didn't have the strength of a real gang behind them. ICP, friends, and their families became the targets of harassment. Rudy's family moved from their long-time home in the River Rouge section of Southwest. Violent J. moved into an apartment with his girlfriend in downtown Detroit in order to spare his family from the unwanted attention.

Undeterred by financial constraints or threats of violence, ICP pressed on. Alex Abbiss, a friend of Joe's brother Rob, agreed to sell *Bassment Cuts* on consignment at his record store, Hot Hits. Right off the bat, he sold twenty copies in four days. That was it for Joe—he convinced John and Joey that they should try to make it for real.

In order to beef up their image as a "real" group, they brainstormed a concept for their "label." Psychopathic Records was born. Joey came up with multiple sketches of a character for the logo, which he loosely based on a crazed newspaper boy who made deliveries in Joey and John's neighborhood. A first draft was the now-familiar figure, holding a stack of papers in each hand. He replaced papers with a hatchet, and the rest as they say, was history.

Next, they talked Alex into becoming their manager and lending them $2,000 to make a real studio album. At this point it was all or nothing for Joe. "I had a purpose…" he describes how he felt at that point in *Behind the Paint*. "I didn't want to be anything. I had worked like fifty jobs and none of them worked out for me. All of a sudden, I had something to do for a living. I was a f**kin' rapper. Failure was not an option."

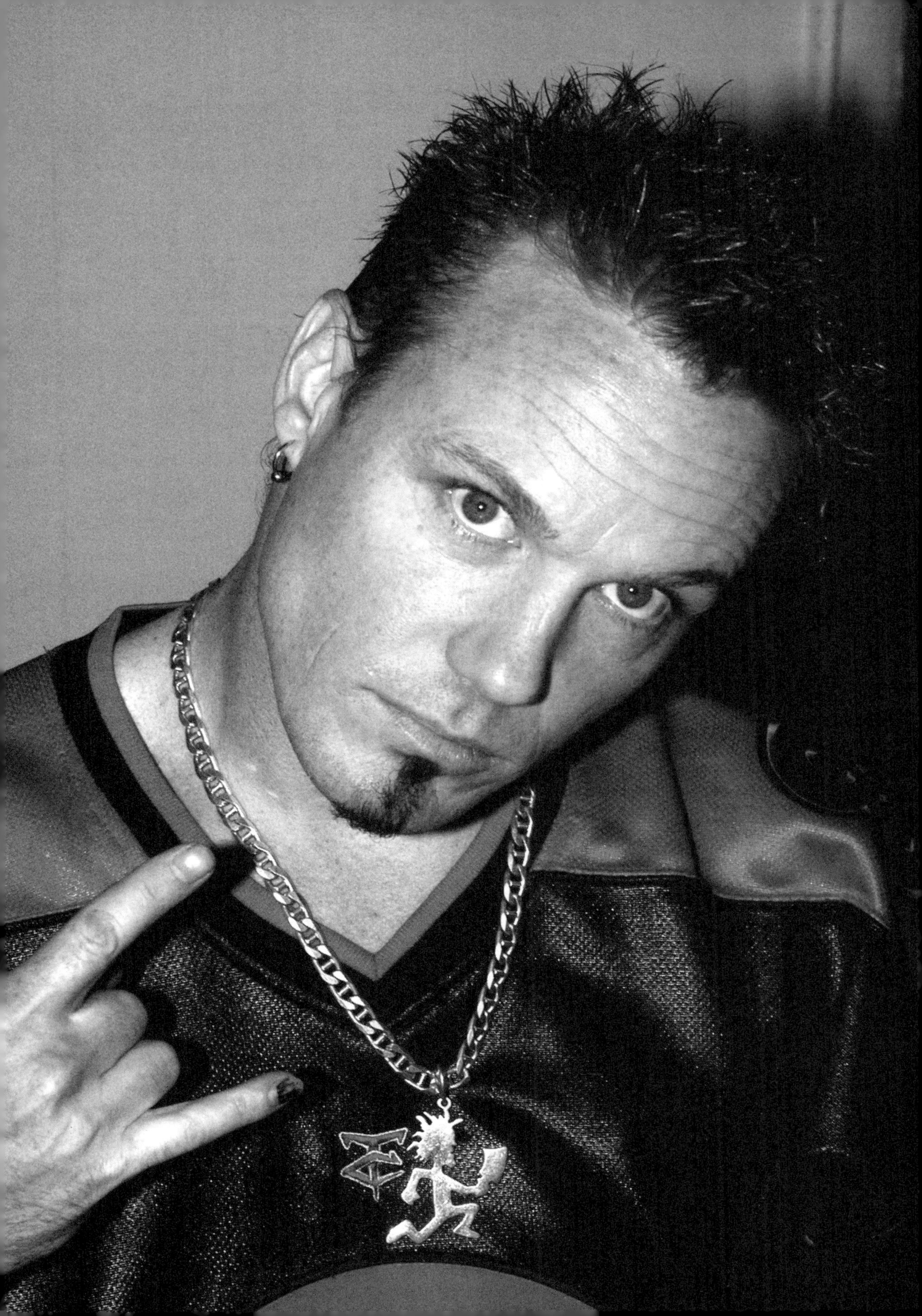

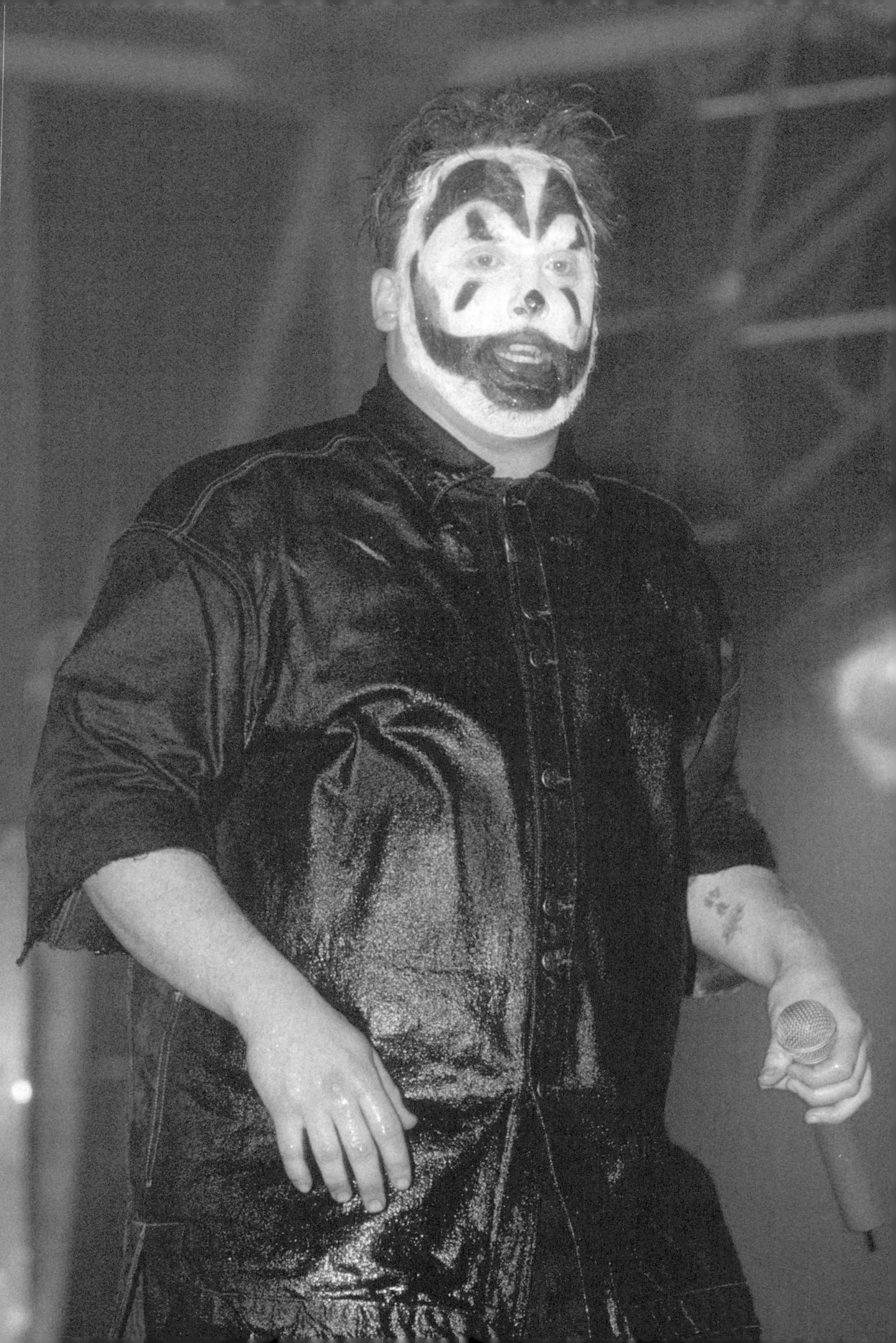

The Dark Carnival is Coming to Town

With backing provided by Alex, ICP embarked on their first studio recording in 1991. They recorded the four-song *Dog Beats* EP at Miller Midi Productions. The songs, including "Ghetto Zone" and "Wizard of the Hood," reflected the crime and gang scene they were still connected to.

In addition to ponying up for studio production, ICP went all out for the cover design for their cassette. The concept was based on dreams Joey was having at the time: A clown running through the streets of a ghetto. Their friend Don posed for the cover image in clown makeup, hanging upside-down from a tree rope in a park with factories visible in the background. In addition to helping out with the cover, Don made appearances with the band at some of their early gigs. According to Joe, he was their Flavor Flav. While Joe, John, and Joey rapped, Don played the clown, running around and doing acrobatics.

They may never have taken a business class, but already ICP was exhibiting a flair for marketing. Promoting *Dog Beats* became a full-time occupation for the band. As usual, they were broke, and had to essentially beg, borrow, and steal to produce flyers and posters for the album and shows. When local Kinkos stores caught on to the schemes they'd developed to make free copies, they would either go to stores in towns farther afield, or would start dating Kinkos employees for free hook-ups.

They placed the album for consignment in as many stores as they could within a hundred-mile

The Story of I.C.P.

radius of Detroit. They placed the album in record stores, gas stations, fast-food joints—any store that would take them.

"We wanted *Dog Beats* to be available everywhere," Violent J. recalls in *Behind the Paint*. "People wouldn't expect a local rap group to have their shit sold, like, in the bootleg tape counter of gas stations. We'd just give the gas stations our tape and let them keep the money, just so it would be available there."

They tried all sorts of angles to get radio play for *Dog Beats*. After months of begging and pleading, they convinced the hosts of a radio show called *Who's the Wildest, Livest Kid in Detroit* to play "Dog Beats." It premiered at 3 a.m., just before they signed off the air for the night.

Alex's meeting at rap and R&B station WJLB would get the band no farther in their attempt to be heard. The programming director responded positively when Alex played their EP for him, but as soon as he realized they were a bunch of scrawny white kids, his enthusiasm faded.

While sales of *Dog Beats* were strong at Alex's store, elsewhere the EP failed to ignite much interest. They were going nowhere fast. There were already too many local bands out there claiming ghetto creds, and besides, no one was buying ICP's gangsta image anyway. If the band was determined to make it any farther, they needed to come up with a better way to capture the attention of the Detroit rap scene and its fans. After all, the Motor City had spawned its share of genre-busting musicians: Heavy metal's snake-wielding freak, Alice Cooper; the godfather of punk, Iggy Pop; and ICP's hero, acid-rap progenitor, Esham. It was time to get creative.

ICP thought long and hard about who they were and what they wanted their band to be about. They came to the conclusion that they should tap into their own lifetime experiences as perennial outsiders and scrubs, and use their anger and frustration about society as a focus for their music.

They knew they needed to keep the initials ICP, but needed a new name that would reflect the change. In *Behind the Paint*, Violent J. recalls that he'd been having recurring dreams about a clown trying to communicate with him, and after some brainstorming, the name Insane Clown Posse came together fairly quickly. That night, he claims, he experienced the vision that provided the band's direction from that point forward.

That vision was the Dark Carnival, which, according to J., appeared as a caravan of strange and powerful beings. Their forms resembled a traveling circus, but he could feel supernatural power behind the familiar images. A figure in the dream showed him six revelations in the form of Jokers Cards. When he awoke, he understood very little of the experience, but knew that he had been compelled to spread a message to those who, like him, needed this otherworldly Carnival's attention. He knew this message would come through his music, and that it would materialize as six albums relating the stories of six characters, and that each one would offer a specific lesson—encouraging

The Dark Carnival Is Coming To Town

people to change themselves before it's too late. The images of these characters would be revealed over time, as Joker's Cards dealt by the Dark Carnival, and the last one would signal the end of it all.

Many people, especially those who are traditionally religious, would take issue with the suggestion that Insane Clown Posse's mission is to provide moral leadership. After all, their lyrics use explicit language and are peppered with references to sex, drugs, and violence. In the band's autobiography, J. concedes that he's not a perfect role model, and describes himself as a "troubled man who continues to make mistakes." He doesn't trust organized religions and doesn't believe in all the traditional Judeo/Christian definitions of sin. In *Behind the Paint*, he explains what the band is trying to achieve with its music: "You could look at our music as fighting fire with fire. Those who never dig below the surface of the music of ICP will probably judge it as a violent and evil thing. Those of use who have dug deeper, however, realize that there is a message that pertains to trying to save the human soul...At the least it's providing entertainment, but at the grandest, holding up a mirror that might help some people to get on a more righteous path..."

Whether you believe the vision actually happened obviously depends on whether you believe in the supernatural or the divine. In *Behind the Paint*, Violent J. relates multiple stories about his experiences of the supernatural, dating back to his childhood, and this is how he supports his assertion that he believes in the vision of the Dark Carnival. Whether it really happened or whether the band created the story to differentiate themselves in the competitive world of music is actually beside the point. The Dark Carnival became the bedrock of the band's identity and shaped the band's artistic direction from that point on.

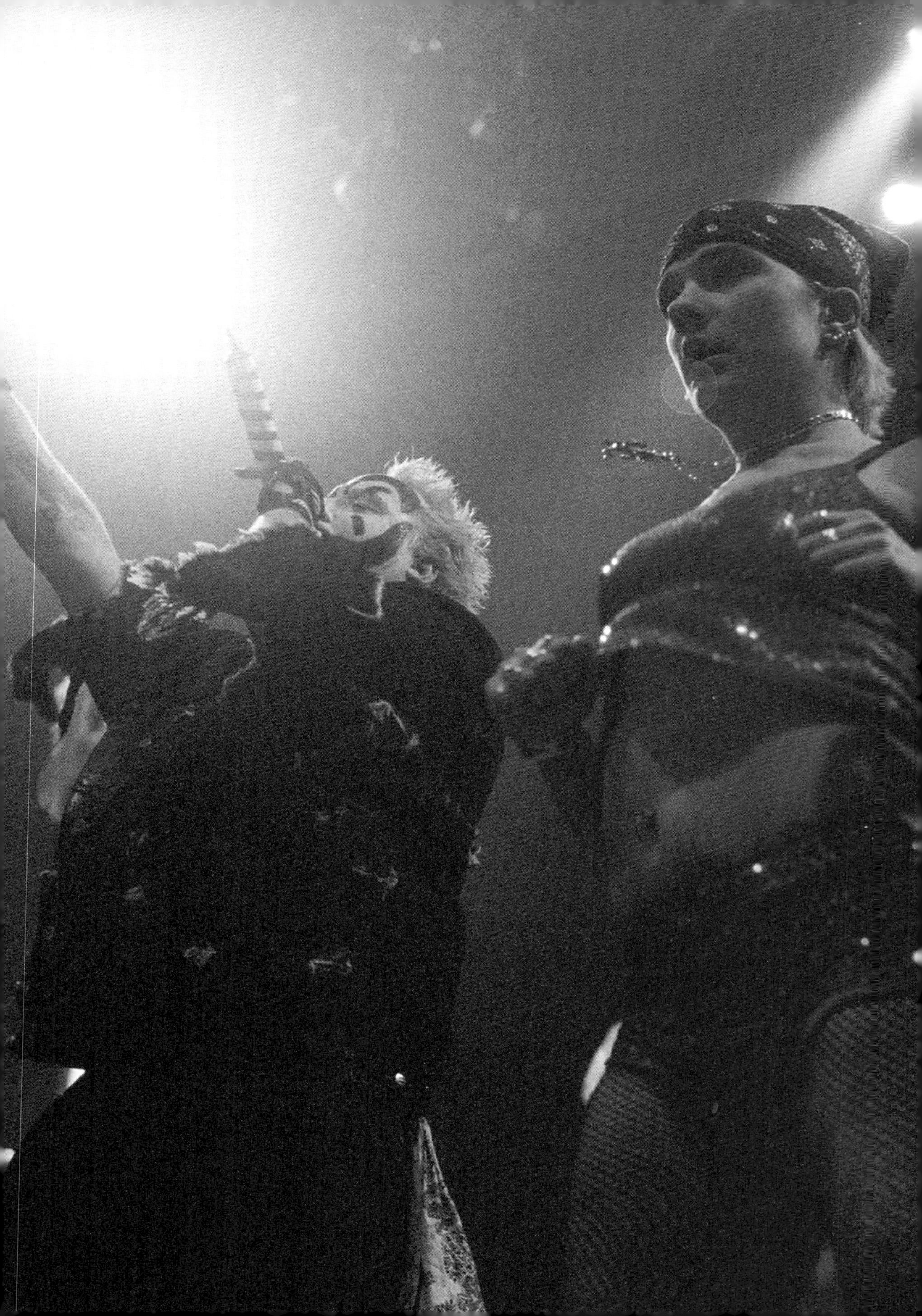

Carnival of Carnage

With a new purpose and a new identity established, they set out to record their first of six Joker Cards, *Carnival of Carnage*. In songs like "The Juggla," "Ghetto Freak Show," and "Psychopathic," ICP presents the tale of a society that has chosen to ignore the plight of the poor and the despised. But just like a circus that brings its exhibitions of the fantastic and amusing from town to town, a traveling mass of social rejects and twisted, angry souls arises to bring the carnage witnessed daily in the ghetto to the rest of society that has chosen to forget them. Instead of inflicting violence and destruction within their own communities, these souls now inflict mayhem on the society that's kept them down.

The song "The Juggla" was the inspiration for the name of the band's fans, the Juggalos. According to Violent J. in *Behind the Paint*, it was a natural fit. While performing the song in concert, Violent J. would sing the lyric, "You can't f**k with the Juggla..." He'd then call out, "What about you Juggalo? Are there any Juggalos in here?"

The nickname took off immediately among fans. From the beginning, they were very loyal and enthusiastic. The Juggalos made it possible for ICP to become successful, despite the fact that the band received little support from the music industry. The band recognized this support early on, and made it a point to return that loyalty in any way they could.

The first three tracks were recorded with their producer from the *Dog Beats* EP, but Alex convinced Joe, John, and Joey that they needed a different producer. They ended up working with Mike Clark, who had previously recorded many local bands, including the likes of Esham and Kid Rock. In the

The Story of I.C.P.

beginning, it was often hard for ICP to book time with Clark as he had many artists that he was already working with, but he would go on to produce ICP albums for years. Clark's music-world connections, especially in the early years, would prove helpful to the band. In order to improve their chances of getting the album into a local chain of record stores, ICP brought in other, more established local artists to record and produce tracks on the album. Both Esham and Kid Rock worked with ICP on *Carnival*.

Meanwhile, the band took some of their first stabs at performing live. As with any new band, it took some time before their music caught on. According to Violent J., at a date with Esham at a local club, the band failed mightily to ignite the interest of the crowd. The 200 or so people waiting for Esham to perform essentially ignored ICP. Despite the setback, ICP was determined to do whatever it took to become successful.

Carnival of Carnage was scheduled to be released on October 18, 1992, and the members of ICP, their manager Alex, and a dedicated team of friends worked hard to promote it. Once again, they blanketed the state with flyers and posters and showered magazines, A&R people, record distributors, radio stations, and booking agencies—anyone they could think of—with press packages to drum up interest in the band. As they did while promoting *Dog Beats*, they spent lots of quality time at Kinkos. This time around they finally had enough money from sales of that EP to pay for the promotional materials they were creating.

Just as they wrapped up work on the album, however, John decided to quit. His contributions to *Carnival* weren't that crucial and it wouldn't affect their sound much to perform without him. In addition, in any images of the band, they were all wearing clown makeup, so no one would really know the difference. Joe and Joey decided to press on without him.

Despite the shock of losing John, the hard work they had spent promoting the album was beginning to pay off. According to Violent J., instead of begging record stores to sell *Carnival of Carnage*, stores around the area were now sending them orders so they could stock it in their record bins. They even had a few fans waiting in line to buy the album the day it was released.

And for their first show after the album came out, at St. Andrew's Hall, they managed to attract more than 200 people. Another friend of the band, Greez-E, donned the clown make up as a stand-in for John. "...the flyers and pictures we had plastered all over the state for the last year showed that there were three clowns, not two," Violent J. explains in *Behind the Paint*. "We didn't want to show any signs of weakness this early in the game, like our band was already falling apart." Greez-E knew all their songs, so it was a fairly easy switch to make. Still, ICP had some kinks to work out in their live show: The crowd was unimpressed with the sequenced robot dance routines they'd honed for their next set of performances.

Carnival Of Carnage

Carnival of Carnage was selling well, so much so that the band was able to use the proceeds to come up with their follow-up EP, *Beverly Kills 50187*, (1993) several months later. ICP once again turned to Mike Clark to produce. Contributions by higher-profile artists Kid Rock and Esham on *Carnival of Carnage* had drawn additional attention and

boosted sales, so Insane Clown Posse once again invited Esham to participate, this time on the track, "Chop Chop."

By the time they booked their next show to promote *Beverly Kills 50187*, Insane Clown Posse was pared down to Violent J. and Shaggy 2 Dope, and the robot moves were now history. The Magic Bag in Ferndale held 350 people, and thanks to more promotional legwork, tickets were sold out by the morning of the show. Key elements that would come to define future ICP performances emerged at this show. Joey took his first stage dive and the band threw their first bottles of Faygo into the crowd.

The Story of I.C.P.

Violent J. threw the first bottle in response to an audience member who flipped him off mid-way through the show. He recounts the seminal moment in detail in *Behind the Paint*: "The truth was, I was winded and tired enough as it was, so I just walked back and unscrewed a full 2-liter of Faygo, and whipped it right at his ass (what happened to him as a result of that flavor is unknown). The place straight up f**kin' erupted, though. The loudest pop of the night. Then Joey threw one off in the kid's direction. Much to our surprise, pop started flying back at us from the crowd.

We kept it going until finally, the Magic Fag's [sic] manager, this stupid bitch, actually climbed up on stage, and in a panic for fear of her venue being destroyed, grabbed the Faygo bucket. Then from out of nowhere, Alex came to the f**kin' rescue, and grabbed the bucket. They were struggling over it! In front of the fans and everybody! Alex was the shit! As Alex held the bucket in place, Joey and I filled our arms with the remaining Faygo, and began spraying the crowd. The rest my friends...is Juggalo history."

While ICP and its fans immediately embraced the beverage's role in their concerts, Faygo's response was more guarded. In a December 1995 *Detroit Free Press* article on the band, Brian McCollum described the company's conflicted opinion:

"The folks at Faygo Beverages' eastside Detroit headquarters haven't figured out quite what to make of the Detroit rappers. Company President Stan Sheridan has never seen or heard the group, but he certainly knows about ICP's onstage Faygo antics.

'Our first reaction when somebody uses our product—and says something good about it—is positive,' Sheridan says. As for pouring Faygo on concert-goers, well . . .

'We're not real ecstatic about that. We love people talking about our products, but we don't know if we want them spraying everybody with Redpop.

'We've certainly never heard of that use before.'

If you've already done the math—150 bottles at 88 cents each equals $132—toss it: ICP gets free Faygo from a beverage sales representative."

ICP established another tradition of sorts that night: Their uncanny talent for becoming enmeshed in drama with other Detroit-area performers. Because of a misunderstanding with Alex, Esham dissed him onstage before the band went on. At the end of ICP's set, Violent J. took Esham to task for publicly dissing their manager. Later that night, Esham showed up at Violent J.'s apartment, ready to fight. Instead, the two talked out their differences and a messy feud was avoided.

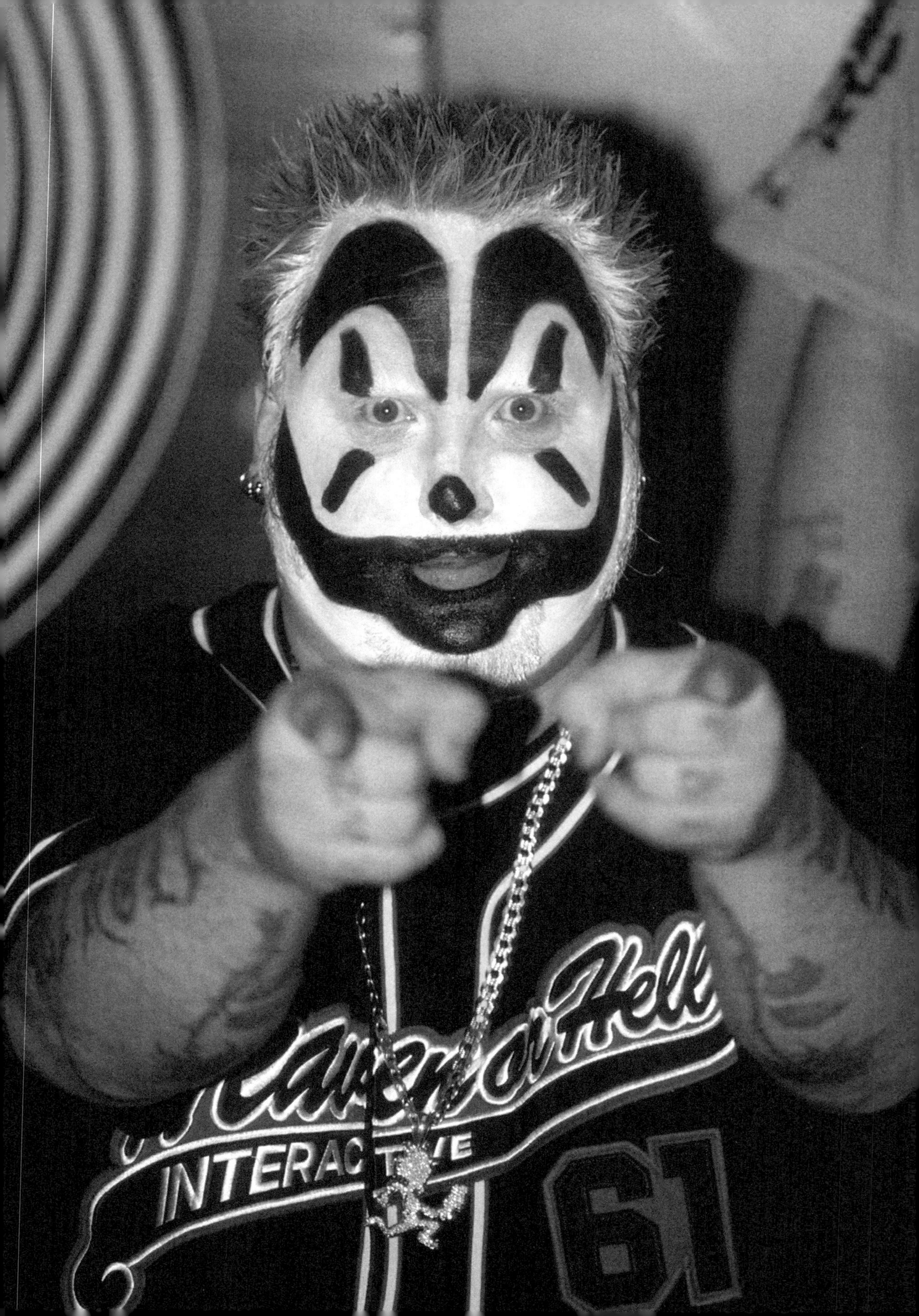
61

The Ringmaster

Their next full-length album debuted in January 1994. *Ringmaster* was the second Joker Card. The album picks up the ICP mythology where *Carnival of Carnage* leaves off. The character of the Ringmaster is the leader of the Dark Carnival. He's essentially the incarnation of all sins and evil deeds, and he is the being that will judge your fate in the afterlife. In songs such as "House of Mirrors" the Ringmaster forces the dead to finally confront their evil deeds:

"Step inside, come my way / This here is your fatal day / You have lied, they have cried / Now your life has been denied / Look into the big mirror / Your reflection is so clear / Devil's head, rotting flesh / With the snakes inside your chest / In the mirror you can't hide / You've been granted Jacob's lide / Whipping fear, spinning pain / All you crying is in vain / You're the beast you never knew / This reflects the things you do"

Ringmaster is considered by many fans to be a classic, in addition to "House of Mirrors," it includes such favorites as the original version of the anti-redneck anthem, "Chicken Huntin'," "Murder Go Round," and "Funhouse."

Once again, Insane Clown Posse and their Psychopathic Records team poured their time and resources into promoting the new album. The hard work paid off, as *Ringmaster* sold more than 40,000 copies within several months. They were able to move out of their old office space (Alex's mother's basement) and buy a company car to do promotions. Despite brisk sales of the album and merchandise, as well as enthusiastic crowds showing up at their concerts, the music industry wasn't interested. They weren't getting local radio play and despite their sales numbers, record labels continued to give them the cold shoulder.

ICP garnered enough support from a few local contacts to get them in the door for an interview with Atlantic Records in New York City. The label's response at the end of the meeting was typical of the attitudes the band would face through their many attempts to get recognition from the established music industry: Their lyrics were too violent and explicit, and their clown identities would never be taken seriously outside of Detroit.

Despite the repeated setbacks with the industry, ICP would continue to court major labels, even as they were building a successful label on their own. "Yeah, sure, we had money now," Violent J. reflected in *Behind the Paint*. "But what I wanted more was to get props on my rapping skills. We thought we'd get it by getting a fat-ass record deal. God, were we stupid. We'd wind up spending years trying to get a record deal, then the rest of our time trying to get out of it. What did we know? We were just a couple of clowns."

Insane Clown Posse didn't have much time to dwell on those issues; they had a local following to maintain. They chose to hold off on producing another Joker Card until they could land a major-label deal. Nevertheless, it was a productive year. In addition to releasing *Ringmaster* at the beginning of

1994, Psychopathic Records produced several EPs, the first was a "solo" effort by Shaggy 2 Dope, entitled *F**k Off*. They recorded *A Carnival Christmas*, a singular take on the holidays that only ICP could have envisioned. The EP included such festive classics as "Santa's a Fat Bitch," and "Santa Killas."

But it was *The Terror Wheel* EP that proved to be a break through, at least in the Detroit market. After some heavy pitching by Alex, local station 96.3 FM picked up the single, "Dead Body Man," and put it in heavy rotation. Thanks to the airplay, ICP was now picking up gigs easily and proving that they could draw their fair share of crowds, even beyond Michigan's borders. At a show at the Toledo Sports Arena, the clowns shared the stage with a line up that included Outkast, MC Breed, and Coolio. The crowd was filled with ICP's face-painted fans.

On Halloween of that year ICP threw the Hallowicked Clown Show, which would become their first annual Halloween show. They held the show at the 1,000-seat Majestic Theater. The Majestic held special appeal for ICP, because not only was it a great performance space, but the renovated theater was known to be the last place famed magician Harry Houdini performed. Houdini must have been looking out for J. and Shaggy, because Jeff Fenster, head of A&R for Jive Records, was at the show. He was eager to sign the band. In an October 1995 article on ICP in the *Detroit Free Press*, writer Brian McCollum captured Fenster's enthusiasm for the band after he first saw them in concert: "'There's a theatricality there that's been missing a lot in the rap world, even in the rock 'n' roll world,' says Jeff Fenster, Jive's vice president of A&R. 'These guys can appeal to people from both of those worlds.'"

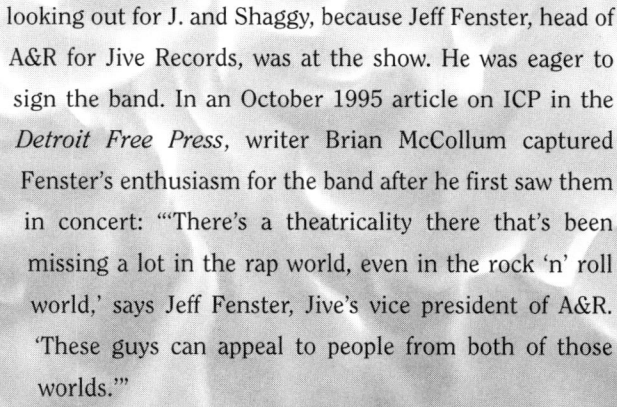

Fenster witnessed the appeal firsthand after an ICP show last year in Detroit. A group of teens had spotted him at a coffee shop, his backstage pass still around his neck. "They started offering me $100 for a backstage pass for a show that was already over," he says. "We think that level of fanaticism is possible everywhere. It's just a matter of exposing it."

At this point, the band had sold 20,000 copies of *Beverly Hills 50187*, 30,000 copies of *Carnival of Carnage*, and 65,000 copies of *Ringmaster*. Despite the fact that they'd achieved these sales on their

The Story of I.C.P.

own, they were eager to sign for the $80,000 advance Jive Records offered them. ICP would finally have the capital to produce a music video. With the backing from a major label, the duo was convinced that they'd finally have a helping hand to achieve national recognition and Platinum sales. The band still had much to learn about the recording industry.

With the support of Jive Records, ICP immediately embarked on their third Joker's Card, *Riddle Box*. The underlying concept for this Joker Card was once again the concept of judgment, and the idea that unless you look deep within yourself while you're alive, you may end up with an unfortunate eternal fate. In the introduction to the album, we're told that when we die, the first thing we see will be a Riddlebox. "A few will see a vision of God as they step forth into eternal peace. But most will witness an image of hell, spawned and formed from their own evil; a hideous reflection of their demented souls. The floor of the room begins falling away as they plummet into a bottomless pit full of shadowy creatures, forever to be lost in a sinister void. What will be in store for you is the mystery, but if you take a look within yourself you will find the answer. For now, you still have time to change the outcome of...the mighty Riddle Box."

Once again ICP would turn to Mike Clark—who now owned his own studio—to produce the sessions. The album would mark the first opportunity that Clark had to devote his full attention to an entire ICP album. At this point, Clark essentially became another member of the band. *Riddlebox* also marked the first time that the boys worked with Rich Murrell, who played guitar and contributed vocals and voiceovers for skits. Murrell quickly became a permanent fixture in the band's studio efforts.

The band's first encounter with Jive's owner, Barry Weiss was likely a harbinger of the quick demise

The Ringmaster

of the relationship. Not realizing who he was, a member of Psychopathic Records forcibly removed him from the bathroom where the boys were in the process of donning make up for a *Billboard* photo op to celebrate the freshly inked deal with Jive. Fenster, their A&R rep, was less than impressed.

Tensions with Jive arose early on in the relationship. The band nixed a new version of "Chicken Huntin'" mixed by a New York team hired by Jive and ended up reworking the song themselves. The video shoot for the song could have been an outtake from the movie *Spinal Tap*.

The premise of the video was that a truck of rednecks breaks down in the middle of a ghetto and an army of Juggalos emerges from the sewers to attack them. The video was shot on the streets of New York City on a very low budget. The band fought with the director to maintain their original vision—he wanted the posse going after the rednecks to include riders on Harleys—but the outcome was so bad that everyone agreed to scrap it for a live performance video.

The Story of I.C.P.

The second version was shot at a sold-out ICP show at one of their favorite venues, Detroit's State Theater. Jive originally asked ICP to play the song multiple times to ensure they captured all the angles they needed. ICP refused—this was after all, a show for their fans. The director managed to get all the shots they needed, and the video is still considered an ICP classic. Jive was none too happy, however. The band had played the original version of the song because their fans weren't familiar with the new mix.

Unfortunately, Jive had the last laugh. *Riddle Box* dropped in the first part of 1995, and, despite a month-long national marketing push by ICP and the Psychopathic Records team, in the first week the album sold only 4,000 copies—no better than their previous releases. ICP soon discovered why: Jive only released the album in Michigan. ICP was furious, but knew they had to work quickly to promote the album beyond the state's borders, otherwise they would never see any money off the sale of the album.

ICP headed to first to Dallas (they picked the city with the proverbial random dart toss) and stayed for two months, building a fan base and convincing area record stores to stock their albums. By the end of those two months, Dallas sales of *Riddle Box* jumped from twenty-five copies per week to 1,500 per week.

Despite these frustrations, *Riddle Box* was making its presence known on the national level. Within a month of its release, the album peaked at #16 on *Billboard's* Heatseekers chart. Eventually, once again thanks to the band's perserverance, *Riddle Box* would go Gold. Of course, it wouldn't hit that mark until the year 2000.

Back at home, the local press was starting to take note, and struggling to define the band for its readers. In an October 1994 article in the *Detroit Free Press*, Carol Teegardin wrote: "I.C.P. isn't pretty, but their two albums, *Carnival of Carnage* and *Ringmaster*, are interesting. They offer up a pounding beat full of so many twists and turns you don't care about some of the blood and gore. And just when you've had enough brutality, they start doing eerie carnival sounds and distorted clown voices that make it seem harmless. What sets these Detroit rappers apart is their vocal style that combines a punk hard-edge strain with old-fashioned melodic harmony. And, they aim to be fun-house weird with their clown makeup and dreadlocks."

After a brief return to Detroit to recharge and to put on their second annual Hallowicked Show for their hometown fans, ICP hit the road again. With no additional financial support from Jive, they poured more of their advance money into their first national tour. They went from selling out venues in their hometown to playing shows in front of forty or fifty people in each city they hit. It didn't matter to the band.

"Playing for fifty Juggalos in another state was like playing for 5,000 to us," Violent J. declares in *Behind the Paint*. We couldn't believe that fifty f**kin' people had actually come to see us OUT OF STATE!!! Every night, we put on the best show we possibly could."

That attitude paid off for the band. Sales for the album increased dramatically thanks to their road

The Story of I.C.P.

trip, as well as the efforts of their Psychopathic Records support crew at home. ICP was impatient to record their next Joker's Card, but they wanted off the Jive label. They had essentially just paid Jive to sit back and do nothing while the band spent its own money to promote their album. Their naivete got the better of them when they signed the contract with Jive, but they learned quickly. The next challenge was to extricate themselves from their label.

Alex had already laid the groundwork for a jump. While Violent J. and Shaggy 2 Dope were on the road, he'd been talking to Hollywood Records about a deal for the band. Ironically, their drive and ingenuity worked against them when it came time to wriggle out of the Jive deal. ICP proved that they could generate some serious money: Their hard work had driven sales of

The Ringmaster

Riddle Box to 100,000 copies, which made Jive much less willing to let them go. Despite the fact that Hollywood had to pay a premium to pry Jive loose from their hold on Insane Clown Posse, they were more than willing to pay it. It took months for Jive and Hollywood to settle on a deal for Insane Clown Posse's contract, but Hollywood eventually made it happen.

While the battle over their contract was being fought, Insane Clown Posse got back on the road to continue to promote the album. At home ICP was a known and popular act, but on the road, attempts to connect with uninitiated audiences were not always successful. A shared lineup in New York with reggae favorite Eek-A-Mouse nearly resulted in the band getting killed—especially after the band soaked the stage, including Eek-A-Mouse's drum kit in Faygo. Dates with Onyx and DAS/EFX proved that ICP wasn't a natural match with the broader rap community.

When they hit Michigan, the other bands finally were forced to acknowledge ICP when they realized the size of their fan base. Tensions still ran high though: Onyx was the tour headliner, but ICP was the clear choice to finish the lineup as the home-state favorite.

In an October 1995 article for the *Detroit Free Press* music critic Brian McCollum provided a glimpse of the problems that plagued band relationships throughout the tour: "And there's controversy even in the home state tonight. Seems that Platinum-selling Onyx, due onstage a half-hour ago, learned earlier in the day it would have to cede its headlining status to ICP. Now Onyx is stalling, still back in its Radisson Hotel room, hoping to force ICP onto the stage. With ICP's image-sensitive manager a few feet away, Violent J. keeps a diplomatic stance. 'We're just happy to show Onyx and Das that we've got an audience, too,' he says, a slight smile coming to his black-rimmed lips. 'I knew I could count on Michigan to come through for us.'"

Insane Clown Posse dropped off the tour soon thereafter. They had more important priorities to address. Now that their contract with Hollywood Records was about to start, they could focus their energies on the fourth Joker's Card.

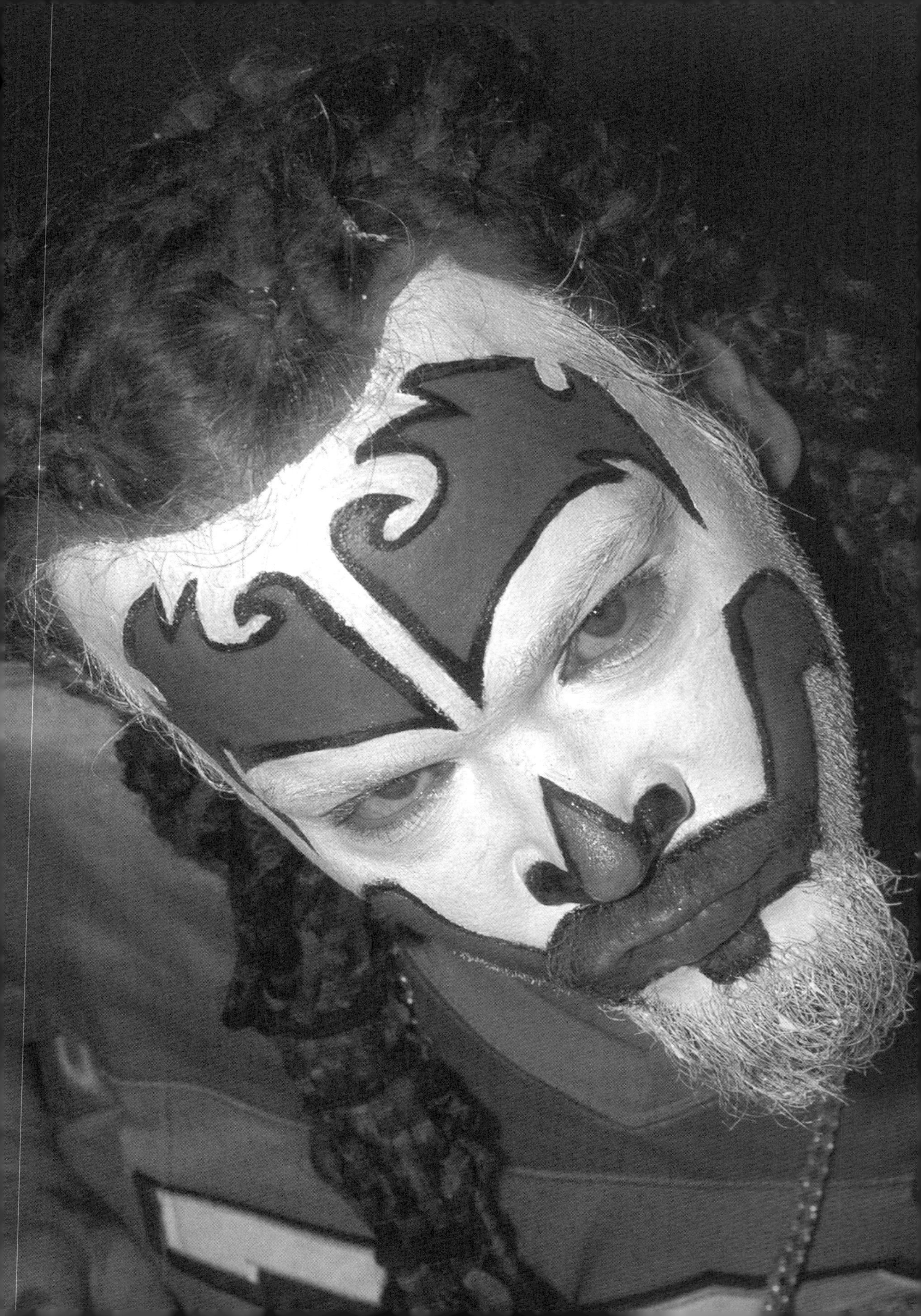

Hellalujah

As excited as ICP was about switching to Hollywood Records, they had one fear that initially held them back: Hollywood was owned by Disney, the mother of all family-values oriented companies. Violent J. and Shaggy were concerned that at some point in the future, Disney would try to interfere with ICP's not-so-family-friendly artistic vision. Ultimately, their A&R rep reassured them their fears were unfounded. Hollywood—not Disney—had total control over Hollywood properties. As an example, he cited the fact that Miramax films was owned by Disney, but had the freedom to release edgy arthouse movies with controversial subject matter.

Insane Clown Posse had about a week between the end of their contract with Jive and the beginning of their contract with Hollywood. So in the interim, they managed to record an EP, *Tunnel of Love*. The tracks on the album expressed Violent J. and Shaggy 2 Dope's unique and twisted takes on the subject of love, romance, and of course, sex. The best part was that all of the income from the sales of both versions of *Tunnel of Love* (an x-rated version included an extra track, as well as a pornographic cover featuring Shaggy 2 Dope and two lovely lady friends—clowns will be boys, after all) went straight to Pscyhopathic Records.

Regardless of the fancy footwork with the *Tunnel of Love* EP, ICP was looking forward to working with Hollywood Records. Their new A&R rep, Julian Raymond, was a far cry from Jeff Fenster. If he wasn't a fan, he at least had made it a point to learn everything he could about ICP and their music. Violent J. had this to say about Julian in *Behind the Paint*: "To this day, Julian is a for-real-ass

The Story of I.C.P.

Juggalo...He always told us how it really was for real. As far as we could tell, Julian wasn't a fake." The performer wrote this long after the troubles that would emerge with the label down the line.

From the beginning, Julian worked hard to get ICP out in front of the public. Even before they'd inked the deal with Hollywood, Julian had booked them on a promotional show with Cracker and Radiohead. Once again ICP's indifference to the broader industry managed to get them into an awkward situation. While they were preparing their makeup before they went onstage, a member of one of the other bands wandered into their dressing room. Billy, a member of the Psychopathic crew, asked him to leave until they were finished their transformation. He refused, and Billy ended up ejecting him physically. It was Thom Yorke, lead singer of Radiohead.

Nevertheless, Raymond was extremely supportive, and the deal with Hollywood made all kinds of things possible. It looked like 1997 was going to be a very good year for ICP. The band's operation moved into a larger space, this time to a giant warehouse in Novi, Michigan. In addition to housing ICP's office and merchandising operation, the band had a wrestling ring constructed and threw wrestling parties every several weeks. Despite the fun they were having, it was time to get down to business.

The duo started work on their fourth Joker's Card, *The Great Milenko*. In this album, the Great Milenko is another Dark Carnival character. He tricks souls into acts of greed and wickedness, and essentially embodies the dark forces that lead people astray: Jealousy, lust, and temptation. *The Great Milenko* showcases the diversity of ICP's moods. From the cautionary tale of "Halls of Illusion" and the caustic and explicit humor of *The Dating Game* parody, "The Neden Game"; to shout outs to loyal fans such as "What Is a Juggalo" and "Down With the Clown;" and the searing social commentary of "Hellalujah" and "How Many Times," they're all considered by fans to be ICP classics.

Producing *The Great Milenko* would be a different process than those of their earlier albums. Sure, recording tracks at Mike Clark's newly renamed studio, The Funhouse, wasn't new. But thanks to Raymond's industry contacts, they lined up internationally known musicians to do cameos on the album. The plan was for Joe and Joey to fly out to Los Angeles to hang out in the studio while the likes of Guns 'N' Roses guitarist Slash, Detroit rock-legend Alice Cooper, and Steve Jones of the legendary punk band the Sex Pistols recorded their contributions.

Unfortunately, Joey was arrested for driving with a suspended license. Because the arrest was his fifth offense, he received a sentence of forty-five days. While Joey served his sentence, Joe flew out to Hollywood to take care of the cameos without him. In *Behind The Paint*, Joe described bumping into the likes of Pat Benatar and Sting and realizing that he was now in a completely different world. "The whole time I was in that studio control room, that big-ass Cape Canaveral-sized room at A&M Studios," he relates, "I was telling everybody, 'Oh yeah, Joey's in jail, but we're all good,' like I'd been

Hellalujah

in a million studios like that. The truth was, we'd never been out of Mike E. Clark's basement. I was like a caveman watching a spaceship."

It was an experience one could only have in Hollywood. Slash contributed an all-out guitar part for "Halls of Illusion," and treated Joe and crew like old friends. Alice Cooper rolled into the studio to record the intro to the album straight off the golf course....in his golfing clothes. Joe met with Leif Garrett, a Seventies teen idol now working for Capitol Records, to talk about a movie about ICP and the Dark Carnival—and ended up discussing Leif's first time meeting Michael Jackson. One night, Joe and Psychopathic crew buddy Billy hung out at an Alice Cooper concert (with a guest appearance by Slash, of course) with Julian, Leif, and...Pat Boone. As fun as it was, Joe knew it was time to get back to Detroit and reality.

Little did he know reality would hit back hard and fast. Several weeks after they wrapped up the album and turned it in, Raymond flew to Detroit for a special meeting. It turned out that Disney had reviewed the album and wanted some changes. They demanded that ICP change offensive lyrics in many of the songs. They rejected three songs outright: "Under the Moon," Boogie Woogie Wu," and "The Neden Game." At first the band refused, but after realizing that Hollywood wasn't going to back down, they made many of the requested changes. The label accepted the revised version of the album.

While they were waiting for the album to get pressed and hit the streets, the band kept busy. They planned their first major national tour, complete with opening acts and tour buses. House of Krazees and the rapper Myzery (who just happened to be the brother of Rob Bruce's then girlfriend, Nancy) would double as the opening acts and roadies for the band.

Despite the tension brewing between Hollywood and ICP over the album's explicit language, the label shelled out $250,000 to produce a video for "Halls of Illusion." ICP had its frustrations with the video: The label nixed their idea to include Slash (who was eager to participate) and the designer's concept for the set didn't quite gel with Joe and Joey's vision of the Dark Carnival. Nevertheless, "Halls of Illusion" quickly reached #1 on The Box video channel and buzz was beginning to build. Hollywood produced 100,000 copies of the album.

The Great Milenko officially went on sale at 12 a.m. on June 24, and ICP and their crew were ready. Joe and Joey signed CDs for an enthusiastic crowd of Juggalos throughout the wee hours of the morning. A local chain, Harmony House, kept its stores open all night to accommodate fans eager to buy the album. At a signing later that day, the bomb dropped: Alex and Julian told them that Disney had recalled the album, yanked their video, and were canceling their upcoming tour. A statement released by Disney executives, declared that the album contain lyrics that were inappropriate for a product released under any label owned by the company.

Many stores refused to honor the recall, but Disney's move spelled potential disaster for the band.

Luckily, ICP had Alex on their side. Displaying the savvy of an industry player twice his age, Alex went on the offensive. He called the *Los Angeles Times* and accused Disney of pulling the album to appease Southern Baptist groups who were boycotting the company because or their "gay-friendly" policies. In the June 26 article that ran in the paper, Disney denied the charge: "'Disney has acted in self-restraint in many other matters before and we will continue to do so in the future, making our own best judgments,' the spokesman said. 'Unfortunately our internal review process did not initially flag the lyrics on this album and somehow it was allowed to proceed.'"

But, according to Marla Matzer and Chuck Philips, the reporters who broke the story for the *Los Angeles Times*, internal sources admitted that Disney's legal department had reviewed the lyrics long before, requested several changes and then cleared the album for release. It wasn't until the day after the boycott was called that Disney officials had a change of heart about the album.

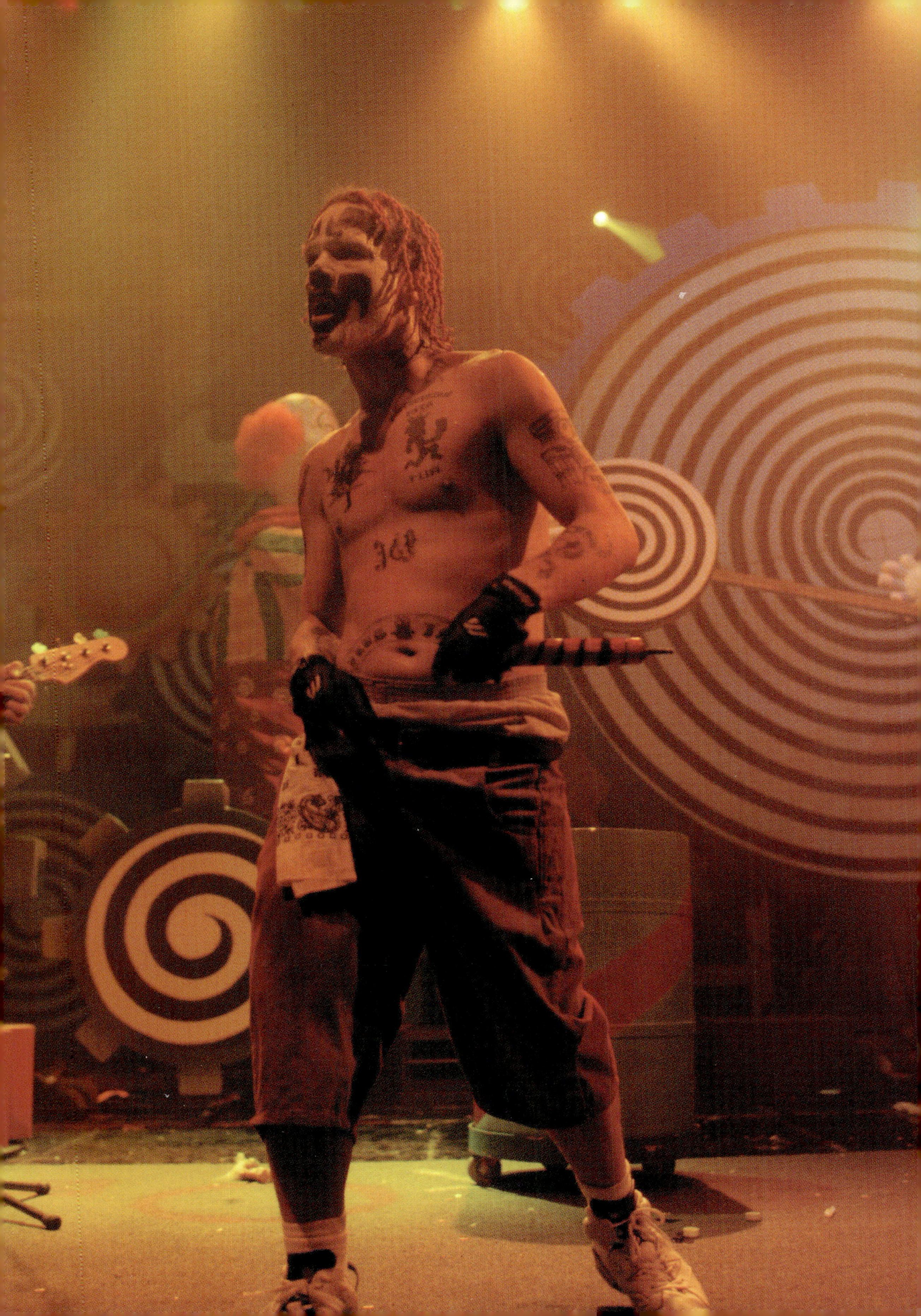

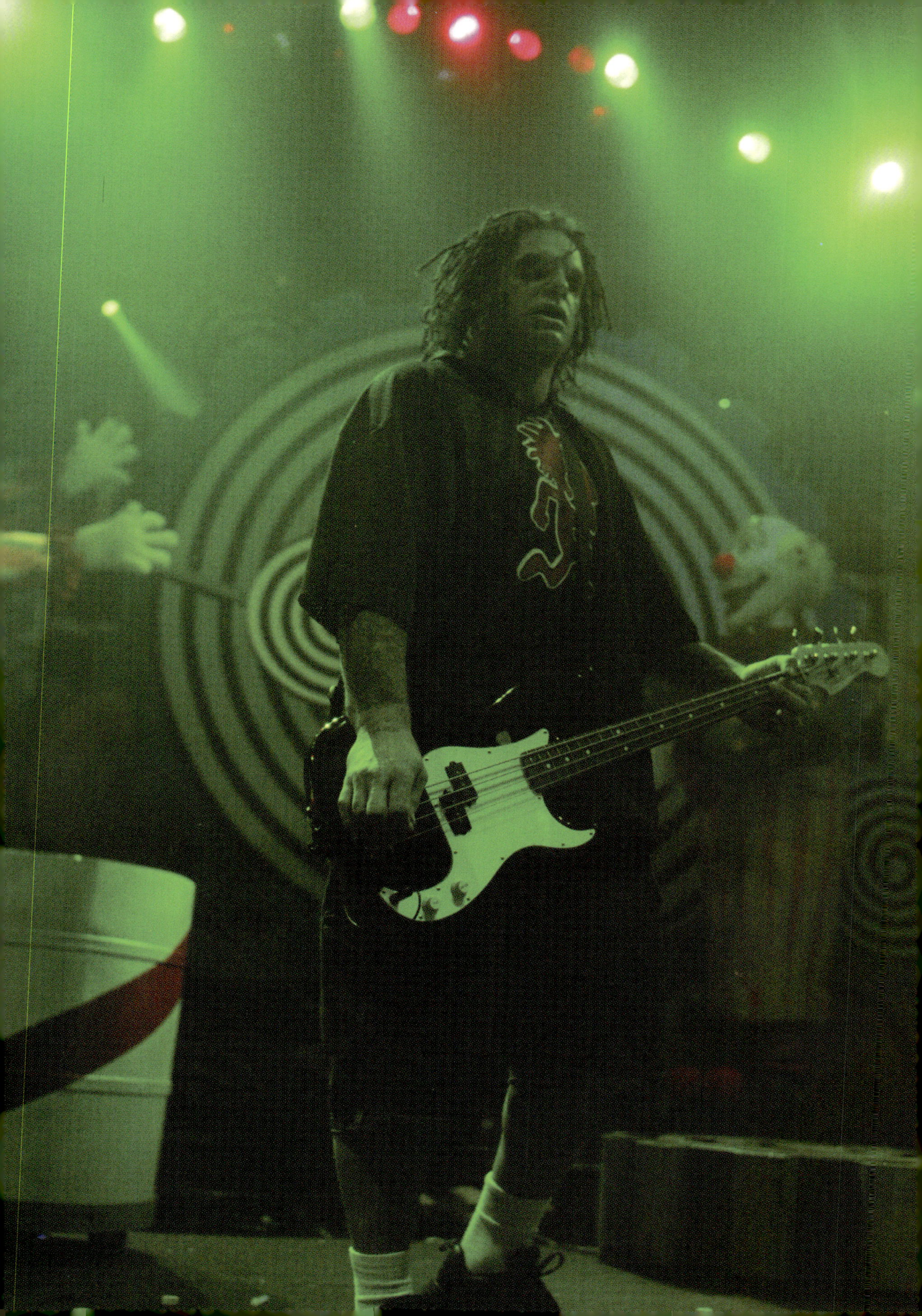

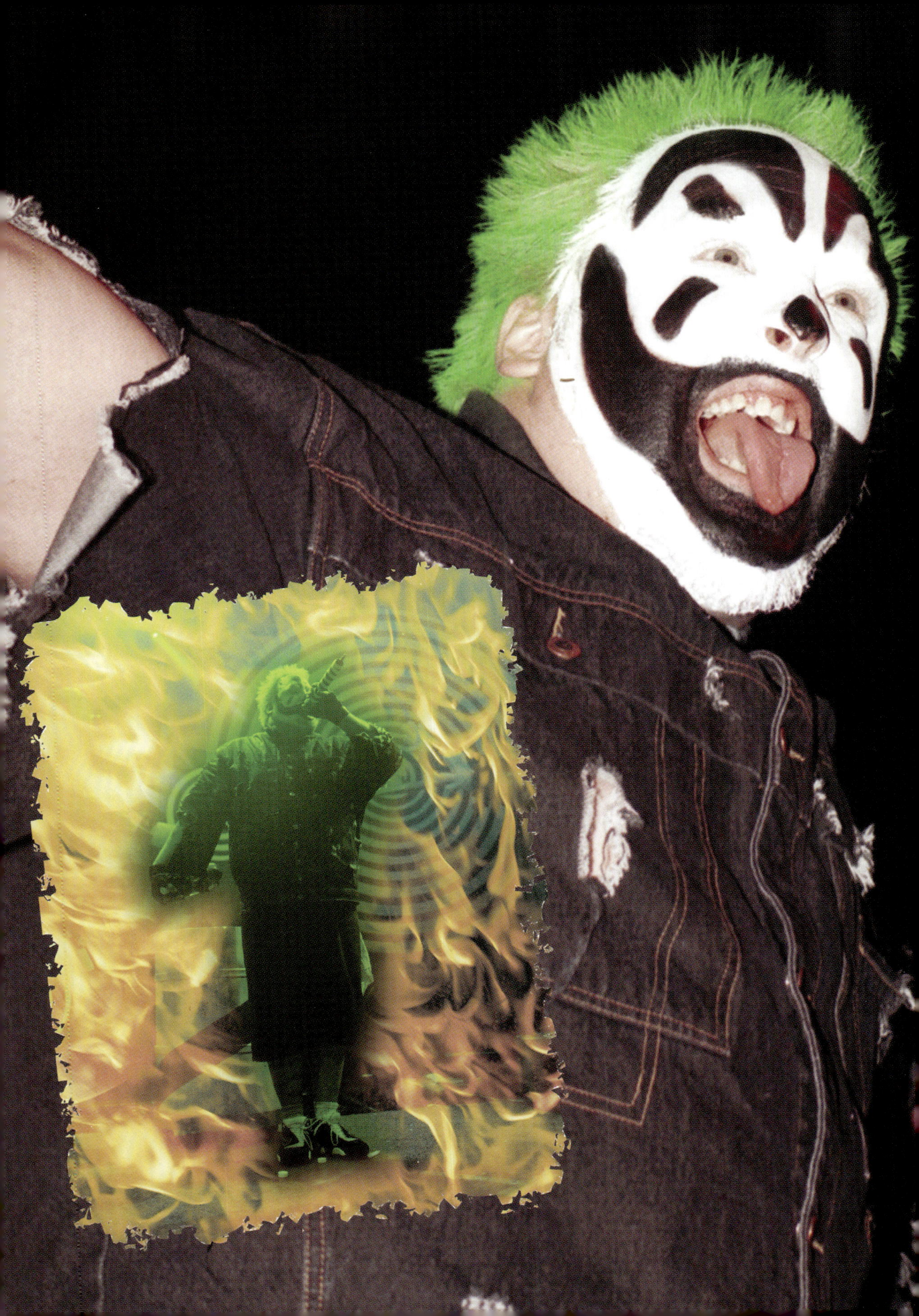

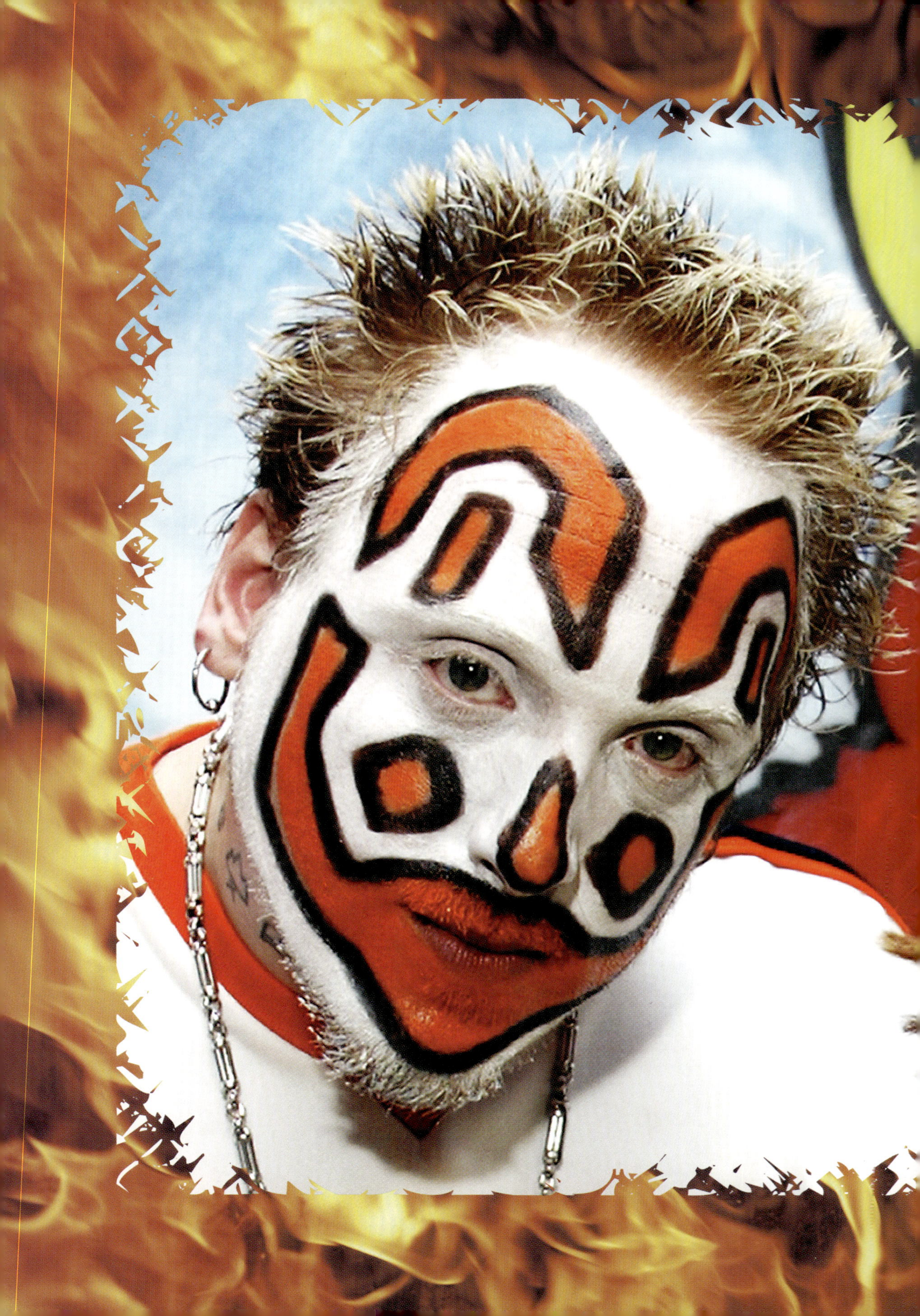

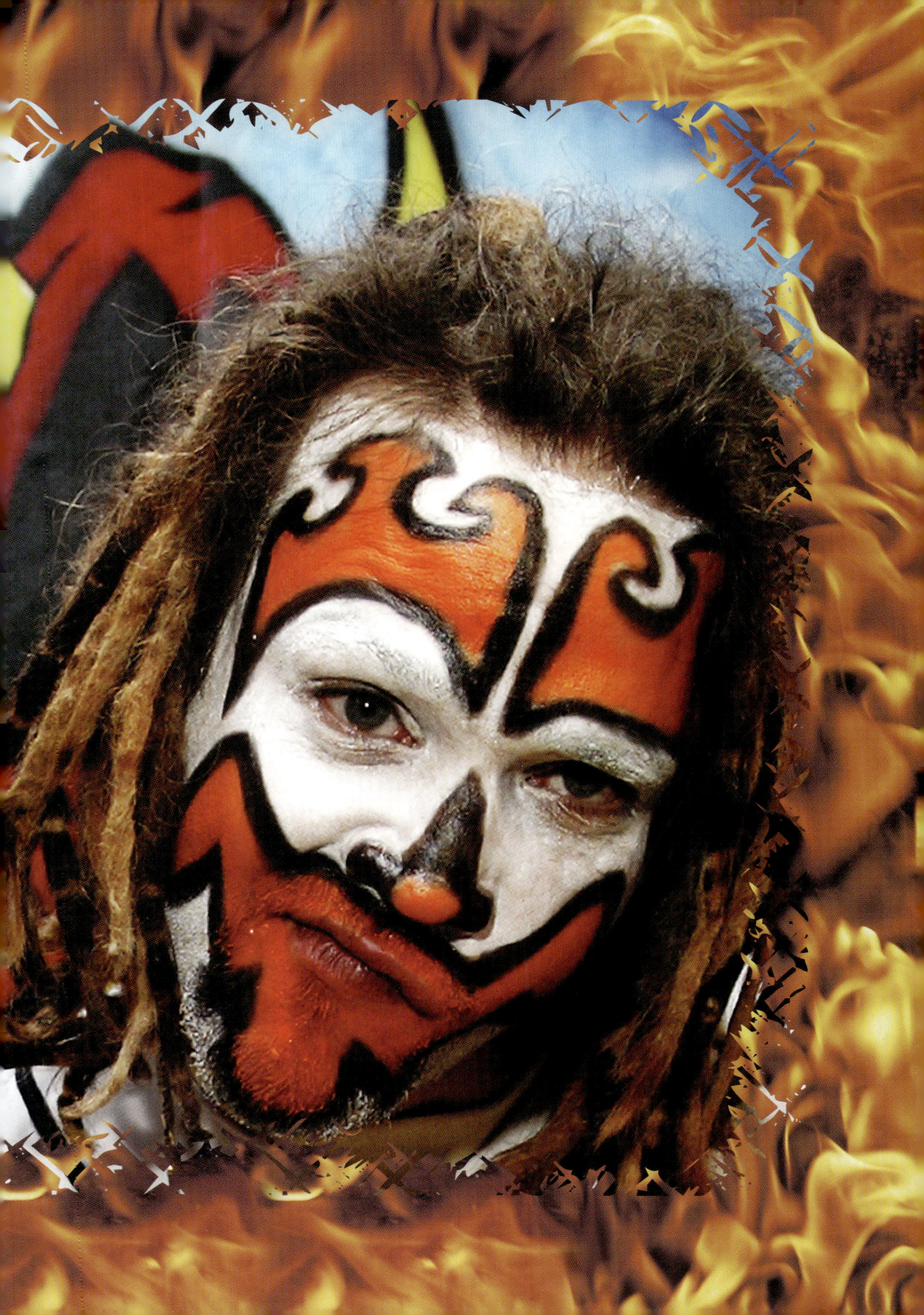

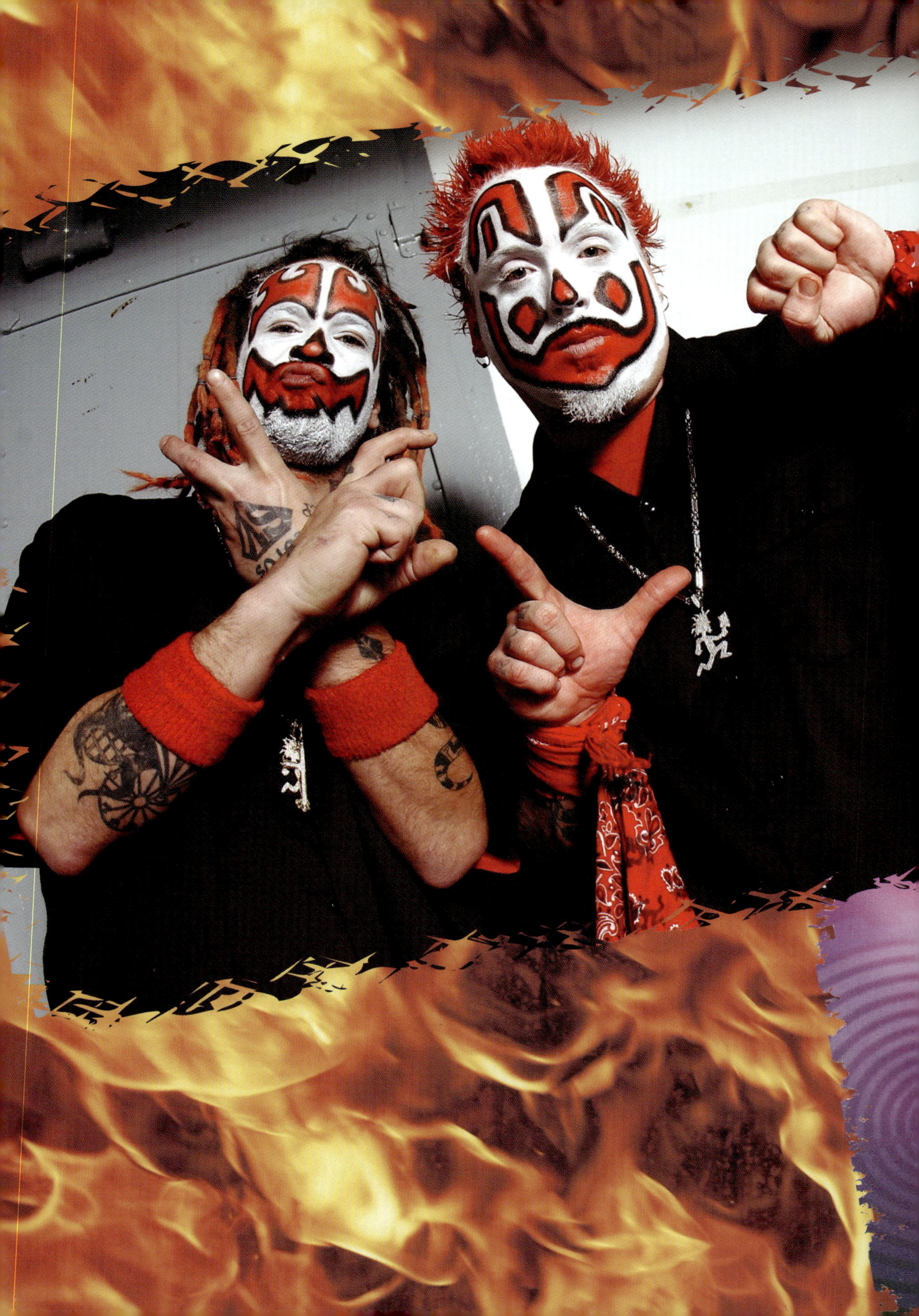

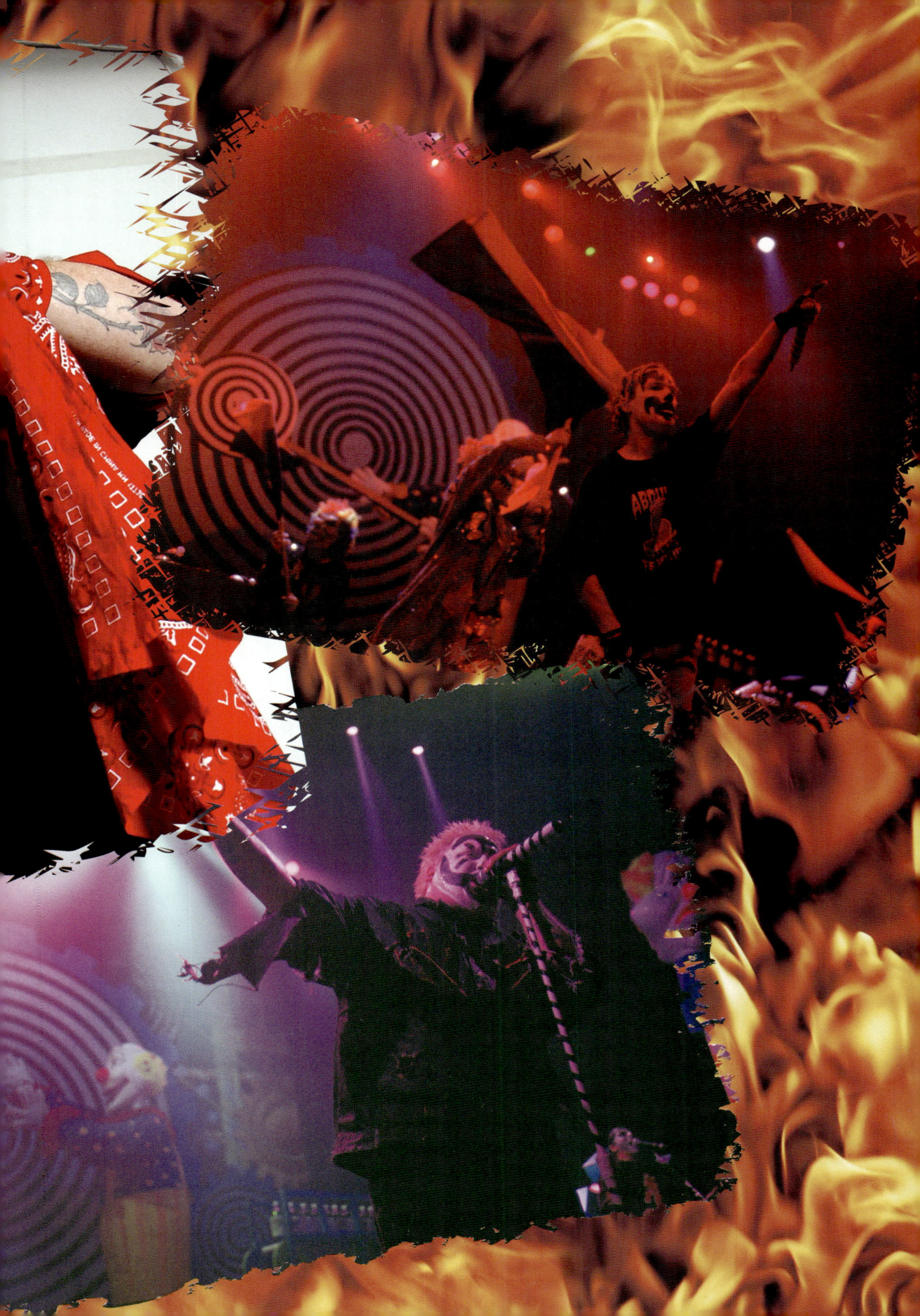

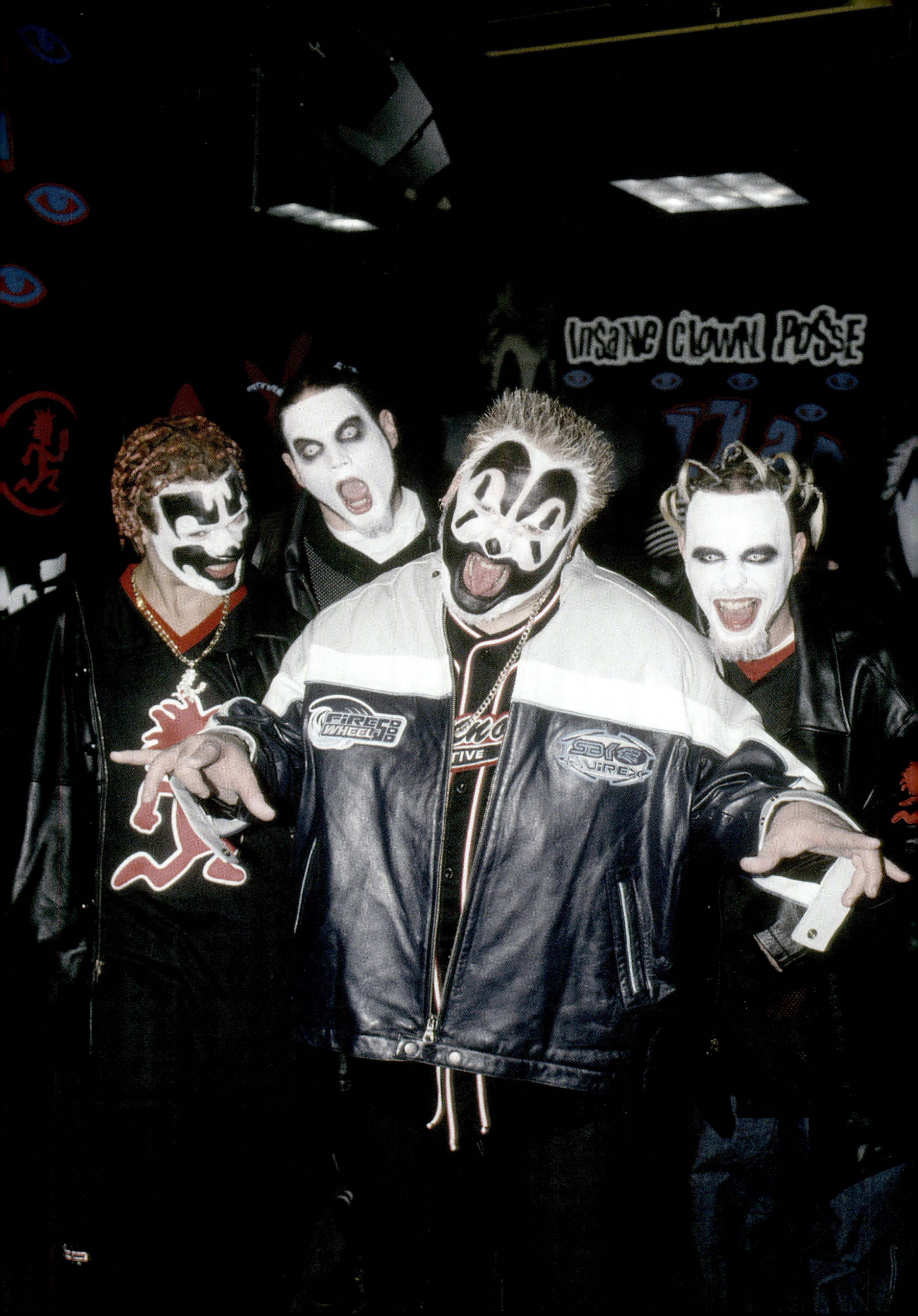
INSANE CLOWN POSSE

Hellalujah

The article, printed just two days after Disney pulled the plug on the album, attracted attention from wire services, newspapers, magazines, and news programs around the world. The media firestorm worked in ICP's favor, attracting the attention of other major labels that were interested in capitalizing on their newfound notoriety and impressive sales numbers. Despite the recall, 18,000 copies of *The Great Milenko* made their way off retail store sales within the first week of its release.

Violent J. and Shaggy became the accidental poster boys for freedom of speech. "...the incident has turned ICP into unlikely First Amendment champions and their album into an instant collector's item," David Browne commented in the July 25, 1997 issue of *Entertainment Weekly*. "*The Great Milenko* joins 2 Live Crew's drooling *As Nasty As They Wanna Be* and the self-titled debuts of the Geto Boys (rejected by Geffen in 1990) and Body Count (from which "Cop Killer" was exorcised) as victims of the sorriest music-biz legacy of the '90s: The banning, altering, or censoring of records."

Some reporters in the mainstream press even took the time to look beyond their crude lyrics, listened to the songs, and found themselves approving of ICP's underlying themes. "*The Great Milenko* turns out to be far more comedic than offensive," reported Marc Allan in the August 27, 1997 edition of the *Indianapolis Star*. "Anyone who sits down and listens to the disc will find that it mocks the rap culture's macho posturing while also trashing rednecks, TV preachers, and kids who stupidly pretend to be gangsta gangbangers. *Milenko* will never be mistaken for great art. But it's amusing entertainment and perceptive social commentary. Anyone trying to find a rap record to pick on wouldn't have to look hard to find something more odious."

First amendment champions or no, the boys of ICP were not about to change themselves to conform to anyone's picture-perfect image. Their live shows were still Faygo-soaked, stage-diving, mosh-pit dancing events, which sometimes got out of hand. The duo often got carried away too, and the results weren't always pretty. After a November show in Albuquerque, New Mexico, Violent J. was charged with aggravated battery for hitting a fan with a microphone. According to the Associated Press, the fan accused the singer of hitting him thirty times with the mic and kicking him in the head.

Alex was fielding offers from multiple labels, including Interscope, Epic, Restless, and Island records. Breaking out the champagne bottles wasn't an option yet, however. Despite the fact that Disney didn't want to be associated with the Posse's violent and explicit lyrics, they had no intention of letting the band walk away without compensation for the money they'd invested in producing and marketing the album.

Insane Clown Posse eventually signed with Island, which wholeheartedly backed the beleaguered album. The label re-released the original version, with all original lyrics and the three additional songs Disney had refused to include. Immediate sales were strong (in its first week out it once again sold

The Story of I.C.P.

18,000 copies), but not as strong as Island and ICP had hoped: They were looking for it to chart at #1. Island's marketing team got creative: They produced an hour-long documentary—err, shockumentary, after all, these were twisted, evil, horror-obsessed clowns—about the band. The documentary, which highlighted the experience of a Juggalo en route to an ICP concert, took on a life of it's own. By 2002 the video had gone Gold.

The tough part was getting someone to show it. At one point, Island won an hour-long slot on MTV at a charity auction. But when they approached MTV, the network refused to run it. Eventually Island prevailed and the gambit paid off. The album sold 500,000 copies in the week following the broadcast. During the broadcast, however, MTV made it clear that the airtime had been auctioned off, and that Island held sole responsibility for the content. Despite Island's jitters, or perhaps because of the extra push it made to justify their decision to sign ICP, *The Great Milenko* reached Gold record status by May of 1998.

By the end of the year, the album surpassed the Platinum mark. While that period presented its challenges, Insane Clown Posse was now in a position to celebrate. The public knew who they were, their albums were selling, and they were making more money than they'd ever imagined. "I made my mom quit her job, and I bought her a house," Violent J. riffs on the excitement they all felt at the time in *Behind the Paint*. "I bought my sister a house. Joey bought a house. Joey bought me a house. Alex bought Joey a house. Alex bought Alex a house. I finally bought a house that I loved way out in the woods, in Novi, Michigan."

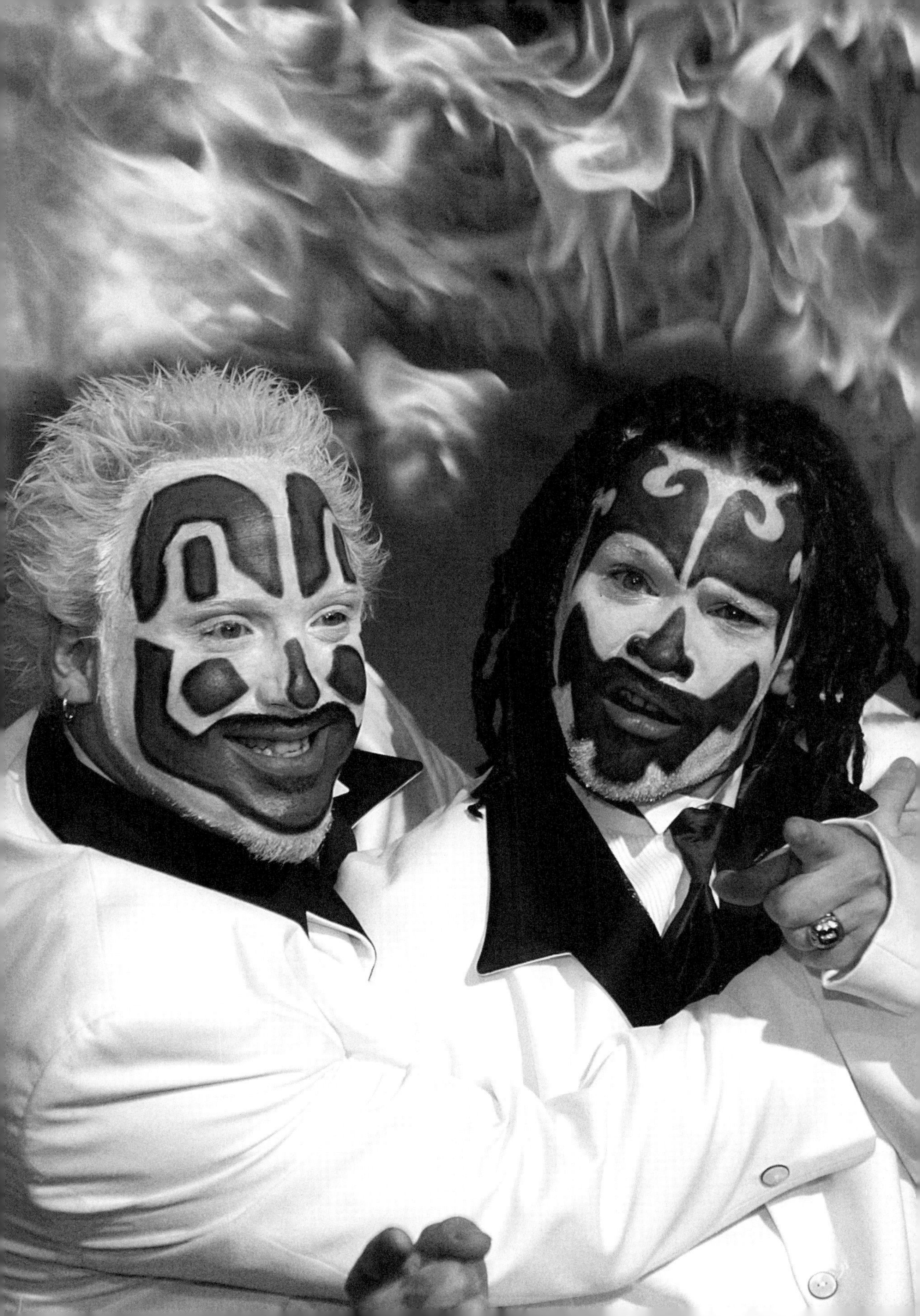

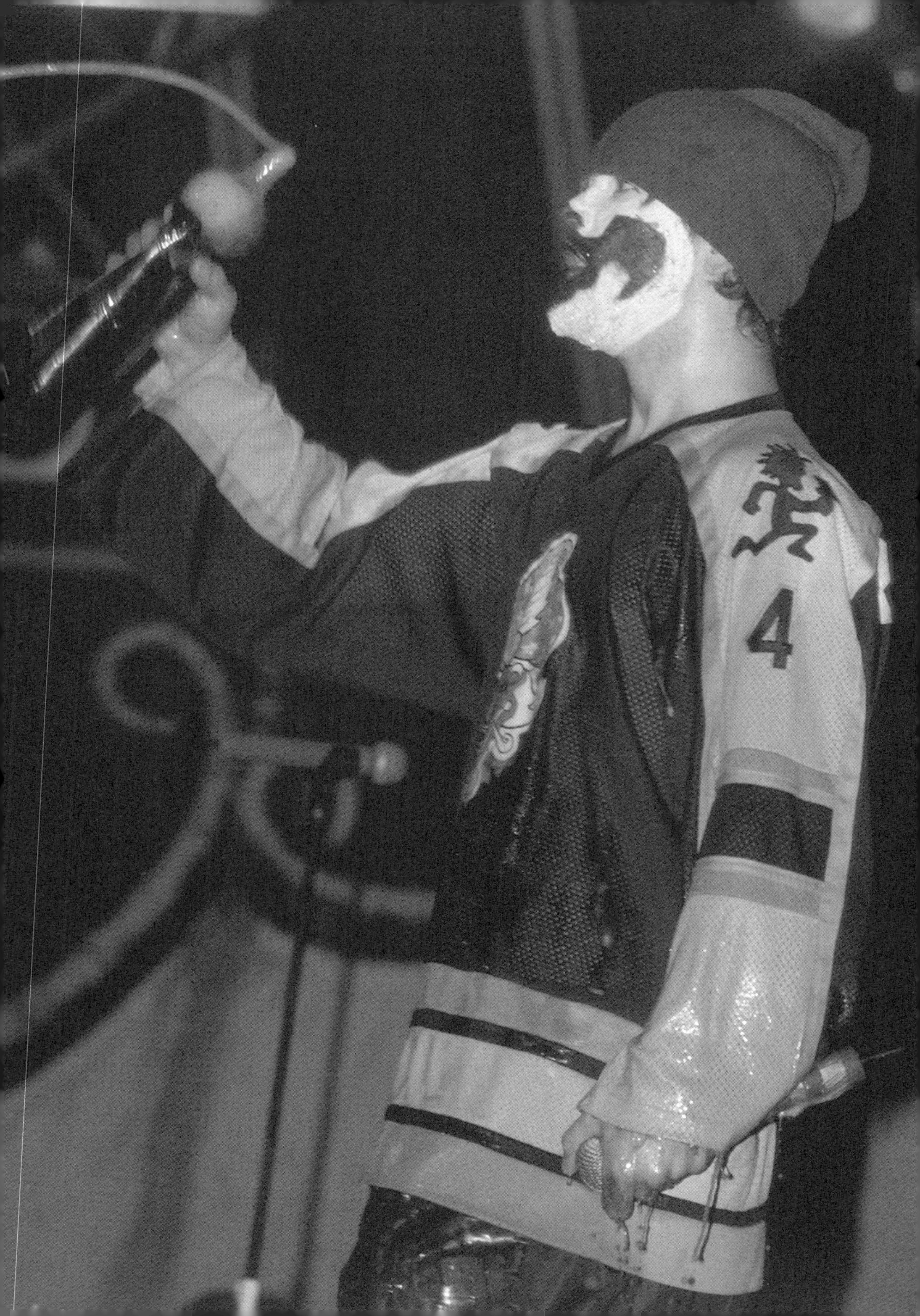
4

On the Road and In the Ring

After the stress of the previous year, it was clearly an exciting time for the band. Taking a break was not an option at this point. ICP rescheduled their tour to support *The Great Milenko*. Before they set out on the road, they made time to support friends from Violent J.'s pro-wrestling past. Violent J. and Shaggy hopped into the ring against pals Rob Van Dam and Sabu for an ECW (a fledgling wrestling association) pay-per-view broadcast.

Just days after the match, the band and their supporting acts rolled out of Detroit in plush tour buses. The first stop on the road was Orlando, Florida. Ever the clowns, ICP decided to launch the tour in Disney's backyard with a free concert.

Life on the road was a roller-coaster ride for the band and their crew. ICP loved performing in front of fans, and the crowds were getting bigger as the tour continued. Groupies were coming out of the woodwork. Fantasies of women throwing themselves at them were now reality. In *Behind the Paint*, Joe describes the scene one night in Dallas: "We were sitting there in the hotel after a bomb-ass show at Deep Ellum Live, and believe it or not, but there was about twenty chicks all sitting outside leaning against their cars, just waiting out in the parking lot. Waiting for what? Waiting to be chosen by us, or by somebody, anybody in the crew, or even on the tour at least."

Later, of course, Joe would acknowledge the emotional emptiness of those experiences, but in the beginning neither he, nor anyone else on the tour had any complaints.

But life on tour wasn't always fun. Band members of House of Krazees weren't getting along, which

The Story of I.C.P.

caused tension for everyone. At the end of the first leg of the tour, the support band dropped off the tour because one member refused to continue. On the second leg of the tour, Jamie and Paul would rejoin ICP on the road, this time as the duo Twiztid.

Between the first and second legs of the tour, Joe made an acquaintance at a concert at St. Andrew's Hall—one who would make occasional unwelcome appearances in the Insane Clown Posse saga in the future. Marshall Mathers, a.k.a. Eminem, was handing out flyers promoting the release of his new EP. On the flyer, he listed ICP among the local rap heroes slated to make an appearance at his EP release party. Joe bitched him out and went on his way. "Who would have ever known what would all become of that one ninety-second encounter," Joe muses in *Behind the Paint*. "That was the first and the last time I have ever met the future superstar, Eminem, face-to-face. He wasn't even famous yet, not even signed, just promoting his new Slim Shady EP, and he was already pulling bitch tactics."

The second leg of the tour was filled with unexpected twists and turns. On January 22, en route to Cleveland, the tour bus was in an accident that gave Violent J. enough of a concussion to postpone two shows. Just eight days later, tour members got involved in a brawl with a local teen, Douglas Jordan, at a Waffle House in Greenfield, Indiana. Ten people, including Violent J., Shaggy, and other members of their crew, along with Jack Gonzalez and Gustavo Gonzalez of Psycho Realm, were arrested and charged with battery. According to band members, Jordan provoked the entourage with offensive behavior and comments towards the group.

Luckily for the bands, after one night in the slammer, the boys made bail and made it to their next show on time. Violent J. and Shaggy's trial took place several months later. They were ultimately hit with a lesser charge of disorderly conduct and fined $325 each.

The tour was split up into three legs, and during their breaks the boys worked on projects with Twiztid (former band members of House of Krazees) and Myzery. Twiztid signed on to the Psychopathic Records roster and worked closely with Violent J. on their first release, *Mostasteless*. Signing Twiztid to the label proved to be a smart move for both bands. Not only would they prove to be chill road partners, they would also be a great opening band. Eventually they would develop a strong following of their own and headline their own tours.

Myzery signed on to the label not long after Twiztid came on board. ICP contributed a track to his EP, *Para La Isla*. A South Bronx native originally from Puerto Rico, Myzery rapped in English and Spanish. While the album featured fresh beats and inventive lyrics, Juggalos wouldn't embrace Myzery as wholeheartedly as they would Twiztid.

On the third leg, the Juggalo Funhouse Tour, ICP added Myzery, Twiztid, and the Kottonmouth Kings to the roster. By the end of April, it looked like the pace was getting to the band. Joe experienced several episodes of overwhelming stress. On April 19, in the middle of a show at the Roy Wilkins

On The Road And In The Ring

Auditorium in St. Paul, Minneapolis, Violent J. literally froze onstage. A posse member realized he was in trouble and killed all the lights onstage except for a spotlight on Shaggy, who carried the show for a few songs. J. got back onstage a little bit later, but they ended the concert early. According to a fan account in an MTV news report, he didn't notice anything was wrong until much later, when he read an announcement about J.'s condition on the band's Web site.

The rest of the tour was canceled and the band returned to Michigan so that Joe could rest. He suffered an even more severe attack and landed in a mental institution for several days. His doctor explained that the episodes he experienced were panic attacks, which were caused by a chemical imbalance. Joe was treated and released, and with the support of family, friends, and drug therapy, he soon got back to making music.

In fact, the European leg of the tour, which started in Paris on May 12, went ahead as scheduled. The tour, which led ICP through England, France, Italy, Germany, and France, among other nations, was a whirlwind. Language barriers, foreign food, and crazy travel schedules were tough on the band. They often had problems with other bands when they shared a billing. But, as Violent J. relates in *Behind the Paint*, their European fans made it all worthwhile. "Even with the small crowd, they were hype as hell," says Violent J. "They made it all worth while being over there...It was so amazing to me to see that there are scrubs around the world who are just like me. They were from different countries, and I never could figure out their handshakes, but in every way they were a part of our Juggalo family, and they get mad respect for that."

Nevertheless, when the tour wrapped up, everyone was eager to take a break from the road. In *Behind the Paint* Joe freely admits being an ugly American. He was ready to get back to his couch, fast food, and Faygo, and, as it turned out, wrestling.

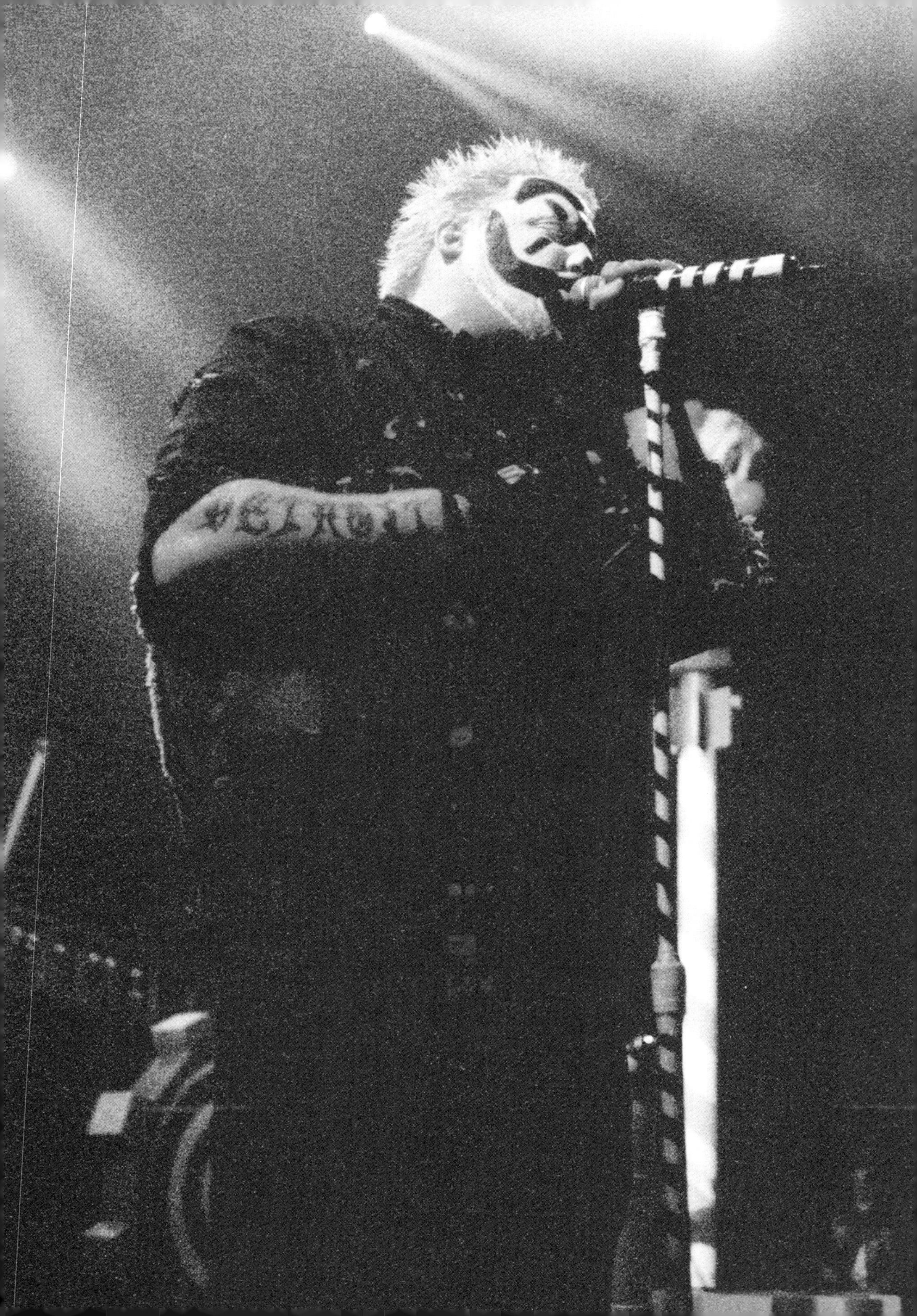

WWF

The band returned home at the end of the month with all sorts of projects brewing on the horizon. In mid-August, ICP released *Forgotten Freshness, Volumes 1 & 2*. In addition to the original set released in 1995, the album included more B-sides, outtakes, unreleased singles, and remixes of old favorites, including "Fat Sweaty Betty," "Mental Warp," "Southwest Strangla," and their Christmas classic, "Santa's a Fat Bitch."

Even before they'd returned home from Europe, Violent J. and Shaggy were in talks with the World Wrestling Federation. The WWF invited the duo—who were lifelong wrestling fans—to perform a song at their Summer Slam event at Madison Square Garden. ICP had already gone public with their love of wrestling. First, they released a wrestling video, ICP's Strangle-Mania, which was essentially bootlegged footage of extreme wrestling matches from Japan. The ICP contribution, in addition to picking the best footage, was to rename the wrestlers as Juggalo characters and to overdub their unique play-by-play commentary.

With the success of the video, they took a step further. That spring they hosted ICP's Strangle-Mania Live at St. Andrew's Hall—one of the Detroit venues they'd performed at as a band. This time around, Violent J. and Shaggy would wrestle as their rapper personas. The main event featured ICP in full grease-paint glory versus the tag team The Chicken Boys (the characters Al Labama and Confederate Fred were played by local friends). Famous indie-circuit wrestlers they'd followed when they were young were also on the bill that night. But with the WWF invitation, they'd hit the wrestling big time.

The Story of I.C.P.

On August 19, just days after *Forgotten Freshness* hit the streets, ICP performed the song, "The Greatest Show," written specially for the wrestling team known as The Oddities. Backstage, Joe and Joey were star struck. They'd spent much of their childhood either watching the sport or wrestling in backyard match ups. Joe had even wrestled in indie matches. They met many of the Federation's star wrestlers, but meeting and hanging out with Vince McMahon, the chairman of the WWF, was the highlight of the day. "Both my and Joey's mouths dried up like the Sahara Desert when we were talking to him," J. describes in *Behind the Paint*. "It was wild. That guy was the one person who was responsible for so much enjoyment in our lives."

If Violent J. and Shaggy thought they'd hit their zenith, they were wrong; the best was yet to come. After performing the song again the next night at a live show in Hartford, Connecticut, the pair got the go-ahead to jump into the ring by none other than Vince McMahon himself. They wrestled their first match against the Road Warriors. ICP traveled all over the United States with the WWF for several months, making appearances on the Monday Night Raw, Sunday Night Heat, and Shotgun series. They were written into plot lines, and starred in their own ongoing feud with Thrash and Mosh, who wrestled as the Headbangers. Later that Fall, they played the bad guys to "Stone Cold" Steve Austin. Childhood dream or no, frustrations with plot lines and tensions between ICP and the wrestlers became increased over time, and the fun of the WWF began to fade. In addition, a promise to air an ICP commercial never materialized. Eventually, they decided to call it quits. Violent J. and Shaggy walked out at the beginning of December. In a band press release, ICP's publicist cited ongoing script issues as the impetus for their departure. "Their portrayal of ICP was increasingly goofy and inaccurate," was Alex's official comment on the whole affair. "They never bothered to listen to ICP's music and see what the band is really about."

At the crux of the issue was a simple fact: Violent J. and Shaggy weren't wrestlers, they were rappers. By this point, *The Great Milenko* had already surpassed the 100,000 sales mark and *Forgotten Freshness* wouldn't tide the fans over forever. It was time to get out of the ring and into the recording studio where they belonged.

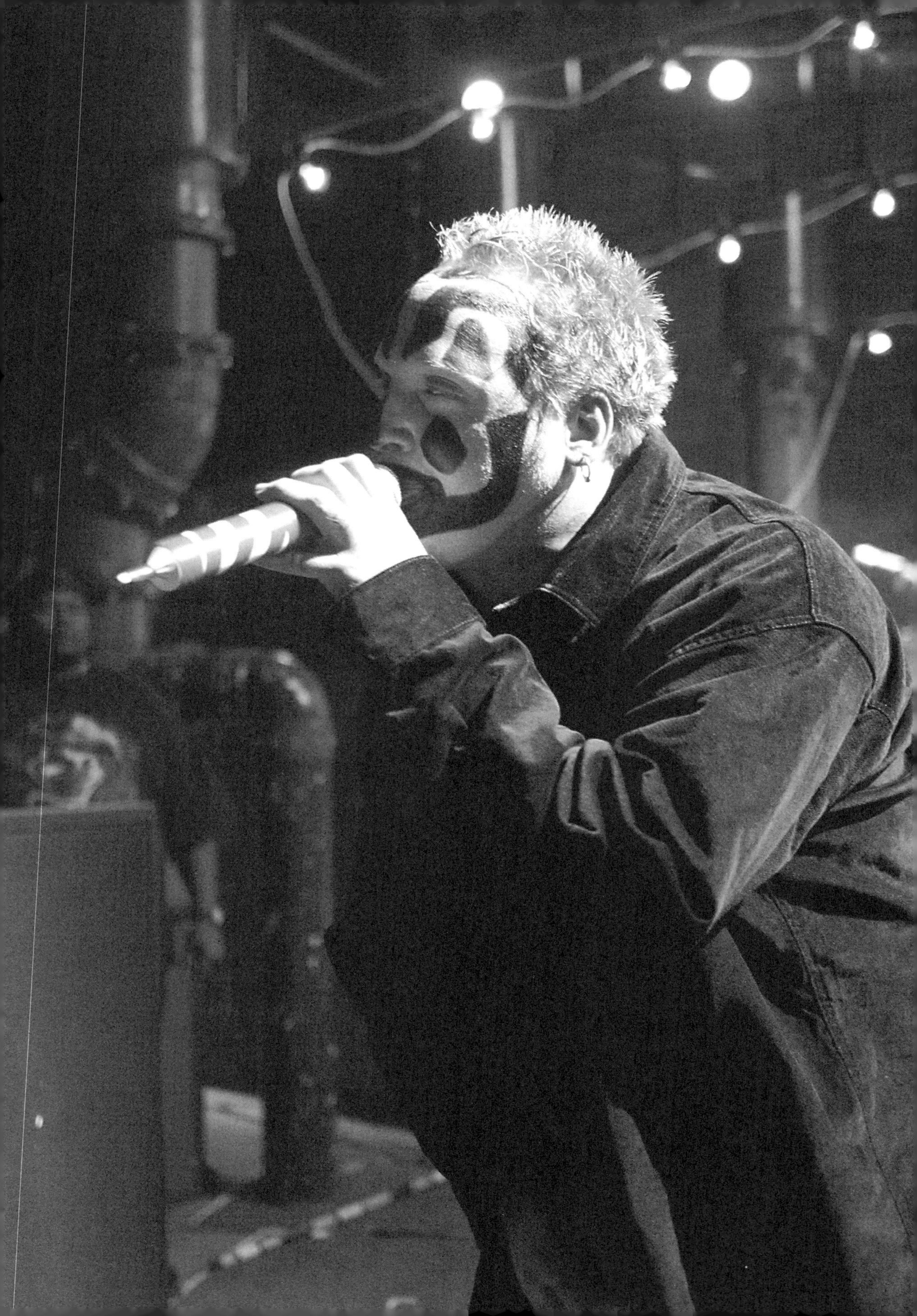

Jack and Jake

Insane Clown Posse lost no time getting to work on their fifth Joker's Card, *The Amazing Jeckel Brothers*. The album introduces the characters of Jack and Jake Jeckel, two Dark Carnival juggling masters, one who is evil and one who is good. They juggle the sins of mortals, and their success or failure at keeping the balls aloft (Jack makes every attempt to influence an outcome of failure) determines whether a soul goes to hell or Shangri-La. In the album manifesto, ICP proclaims, "Jack and Jake Jeckel rest in all of us for they are the very fabric of our being conscience and soul. There is no escape from their Juggling act because there is no way to escape from ourselves."

Once again, ICP brought other artists in to contribute to the production of the album. This time, they tapped gangsta-rap luminaries Ice-T ("Dead End"), Ol' Dirty Bastard ("Bitches"), and Snoop Dog (on the comedy skit, "The Shaggy Show"), as well as famed pranksters, the Jerky Boys to perform cameos. The seventeen-track CD included a cover of "Assassins" by ICP heroes and horror-core progenitors, The Geto Boys. The album was a typical ICP showcase, a mix of good beats, violent lyrics, and biting social commentary. Jeckel Brothers reflected the clowns' mood at the time, and according to Violent J.'s recollection of the time in *Behind the Paint*, it wasn't pretty. "We were angry making *The Amazing Jeckel Brothers*, because that was our way to tell everybody who doubted us during the whole Disney thing to f**k off," J. explains. "We showed it in songs like "F**k the World"; just sick shit that was saying straight-up what was on our minds."

Clearly those recent run-ins were on their mind in the track, "Terrible," in which ICP schools a few

The Story of I.C.P.

choice targets. First up is the mainstream media for churning out meaningless celebrity gossip instead of reporting significant news stories. But strongest lyrics are their ironic take on the religious right's misplaced energies:

"LOOOORRDY-lord have we got a protest, man / Some rock-and-roll ninja bit the head off a bat / Was watching his concert, and channeled to hell / 'Cuz he's so f**king TEERRRIBLE

Meanwhile his records sell double and triple / 'Cuz of you crying about him rubbing his nipple / Religious? Shit, you helped them bang / Instead of helping them poor people eating out of them garbage cans / When you're done with them bitch, come protest me / Shit, motherf**ker I could use some money

"F**k the World" projected the same anger, but in this case, doled it out to just about everyone and everything. The song was an instant Juggalo classic. The lyrics are typically explicit and juvenile, and nowhere near politically correct—but the beat is catchy, and the simplicity of the lyrics makes it stick in your mind.

"F**k you f**k me f**k us / F**k Tom f**k Mary f**k Gus / F**k Darius / F**k the west coast, and f**k everybody on the east / Eat shit and die, or f**k off at least"

Where else would you find the Beastie Boys, the Dalai Lama, Oprah, Celine Dion, Dionne Warwick, Lyle Lovett, Ted Nugent, Tom Petty, Forrest Gump, the victims of the Titanic, and some guy who operates a drawbridge in Detroit called out in the same song?

Oddly, despite the fact that the word, f**k, was used nearly eighty times in the song, Island sent it out to radio stations across the country in hopes that it would be played. Regardless of the fact that the majority of the words had to be obfuscated to avoid indecency fines, stations were able to produce an edited version, and "F**k the World" managed to get some radio airplay.

Thanks to the introduction to a broad swath of media the flap over *The Great Milenko* caused, music journalists were very aware of ICP and ready to cast their opinion on their newest release. While many were dismissive and vehemently critical of *Jeckel Brothers*, some reviewers, most notably venerable rock critic Dave Marsh casually approved. In his review for the October 1999 issue of *Playboy*, Marsh wrote: "Insane Clown Posse aren't just hip-hop's answer to Beavis and Butt-head. *The Amazing Jeckel Brothers* (Island) proves they're better than that. They fuse influences ranging from Ted Nugent's "Cat Scratch Fever" to Iggy's "No Fun" to Funkadelic's "America Eats Its Young." Which is to say they're shamelessly exploitative, but also a lot smarter than they want any outsider to figure out. 'Teacher thinks I got bombs in my locker' is something they would have said regardless of the headlines, and 'I Stab People' is included precisely to attract the censors' righteous wrath. Their masterpiece, 'F**k the World,' expresses a view as clearly as 'Born to Run' does. Listen up or go f**k yourself, they don't care."

Of course, they wouldn't be ICP if they didn't piss someone important off, especially with that song. As it happened, at the time they were recording tracks for *The Amazing Jeckel Brothers*, they used a

The Story of I.C.P.

publicist who also had the Beastie Boys as long-time clients. The publicist asked them to remove the references in the song to the Beastie Boys and the Dalai Lama (The Beastie Boys support his work).

In *Behind the Paint*, Violent J. recounts his reaction: "We had already changed our shit once for some record-company bullshit that blew up in my f**king face, and now some asshole publicity company that we were paying, wanted us to change our shit? F**k that."

ICP adamantly refused and that was the end of that relationship. With their album in production and another music-industry bridge successfully burned, Violent J. and Shaggy moved on to other projects that were waiting in the wings. In addition to a spring release for the album, Chaos! Comics would release the first two issues of the comic-book series, *Where Darkness Dwells*. Joe's brother Rob, a.k.a. Jumpsteady, wrote what would become a twelve-book series. Violent J. and Shaggy would also make their debut as collectible action figures (both in full makeup, complete with an axe for J. and a silver skull topped cane for Shaggs) that spring. Fans seemed receptive, according to a November '98 MTV report. "Kiss had some dolls way back when, so I think this isn't such a shock," responded a young ICP fan, Bryan Elliott. "I'll probably pick them up because I'm such a huge fan. And if the Kiss dolls are any indication, the ICP figures will be worth some money further down the line."

Big-time professional wrestling, comic books, figurines, recording an album—some might call them over-achievers, but Violent J. and Shaggy 2 Dope, just didn't have enough to keep them busy. Perhaps inspired by their recent stint in the World Wrestling Foundation, the performers started planning concepts for a movie. The original plan was to shoot using a camcorder, but Island initially pitched in $250,000 for the project.

The Big Money Hustlas plot was a basic cops-and-mobsters showdown. A good cop (Shaggy) avenges the death of his girlfriend by bringing down corrupt cops and a mafia boss (Violent J.). In addition to star turns from the usual suspects with Psychopathic Records, cast members included the Jerky Boys, wrestler Mic Foley, comedian Rudy Ray Moore, Fred Barry (Rerun from the '70s TV series, Good Times), Harland Williams, and Jerry Only (a member of the punk band, The Misfits). Shooting started in early 1999, but the straight-to-video film wasn't released for sale until July 2000.

The Amazing Jeckel Brothers hit record stores on May 25 and made its debut at #4 on the *Billboard* 200 chart. Within two weeks it had dropped down to #14, but sales remained strong. ICP produced a video for "Another Love Song." While it didn't get MTV play, radio stations picked up the single. Eventually the album went Platinum.

For the first several years of their contract, their record label was very supportive of the band (why else would they give the green light to a project like *Big Money Hustlas*?) But in the first half of 1999, ICP started feeling the aftershocks from the biggest merger in the history of the music industry.

As a result of this mega-restructuring, Island records and Def Jam records became one entity, and the A&R team that signed ICP was laid off.

The change was immediately apparent. "The entire brand-new staff of Island/Def Jam wanted no part of ICP," Joe describes in *Behind the Paint*. "It didn't matter what we sold, nobody wanted to get behind us. They had so many other multi-Platinum artists to worry about that we got buried under everybody's shit on everybody's desk. Nobody was looking for us, either."

In truth, ICP's experiences mirrored that of many artists under the nascent Universal Music Group umbrella. Underdog or top dog, they were all getting the shaft. Six months after the merger went through, Andrew Essex described the aftermath for the July 23 issue of *Entertainment Weekly*: "But there is distinct evidence that the retained talent is feeling alienated. At February's Grammy Awards, Sheryl Crow publicly decried the demise of her former label, which signed her in 1991 and nurtured her to stardom. 'A&M is now no longer,' she said. UMG insists that Crow is 'wrong. Sheryl's albums will be on A&M.' But even if the label on Crow's disc says A&M, most of the individuals who helped her grow are no longer there."

The Story of I.C.P.

Multinational mergers aside, ICP didn't have to look much farther than their own backyard for a reason to get annoyed. In his 1999 debut Slim Shady, Eminem fired the first volley in a feud that would escalate from exchanges of lyrical disses to off-color onstage skits, to assault charges.

Spring 1999: Eminem calls out ICP in the song "Till Hell Freezes Over," with lyrics that seem to directly referenc the incident where Violent J. schooled him for using ICP's name (without asking first) to draw people to his EP release party.

On a radio show appearance shortly after, ICP performed an explicit parody of Eminem's "My Name Is," entitled, "Slim Anus."

Next, Eminem featured an explicit skit portraying ICP as homosexuals on the *Marshall Mathers* LP. During his 2000 summer tour in support of the album, brought up two blow-up sex doll clown effigies and, as MTV news later succinctly described it, "simulated them performing sexual acts on each other."

On the double album *Bizaar/Bizzaar*, ICP featured the song, "Please Don't Hate Me, " at the end of which, Violent J. and Shaggy kill Eminem.

That summer, tensions increased dramatically when Eminem pulled a gun on ICP employee and friend Douglas Dial. The gun was unloaded, but the rapper was slapped with felony charge of carrying

Jack And Jake

a concealed weapon and a lesser charge of brandishing a firearm in public. A year later, an Oakland County, Michigan judge sentenced him to a year of probation and community service.

On the 2001 *Forgotten Freshness, Vol. 3* compilation, ICP took Eminem to task for his behavior on a track entitled, "Nuttin' But a Bitch Thang."

In May 2001, a month before Eminem's sentence, William Dial, brother of Eminem's adversary the previous year, was charged with misdemeanor assault and battery for allegedly trying to choke an Eminem fan attending an ICP concert in Omaha, Nebraska. Dial claimed that he was merely trying to escort the fan out of the club. Dial pled guilty to a lesser charge of disorderly conduct and paid a fine of $100.

All in a day's work if you're a rapper from Detroit? While all this was going down in the background, no doubt both Eminem and Insane Clown Posse were actually working on interesting projects. Let's back up to the Spring of '99 and see what Violent J. and Shaggy were up to, shall we?

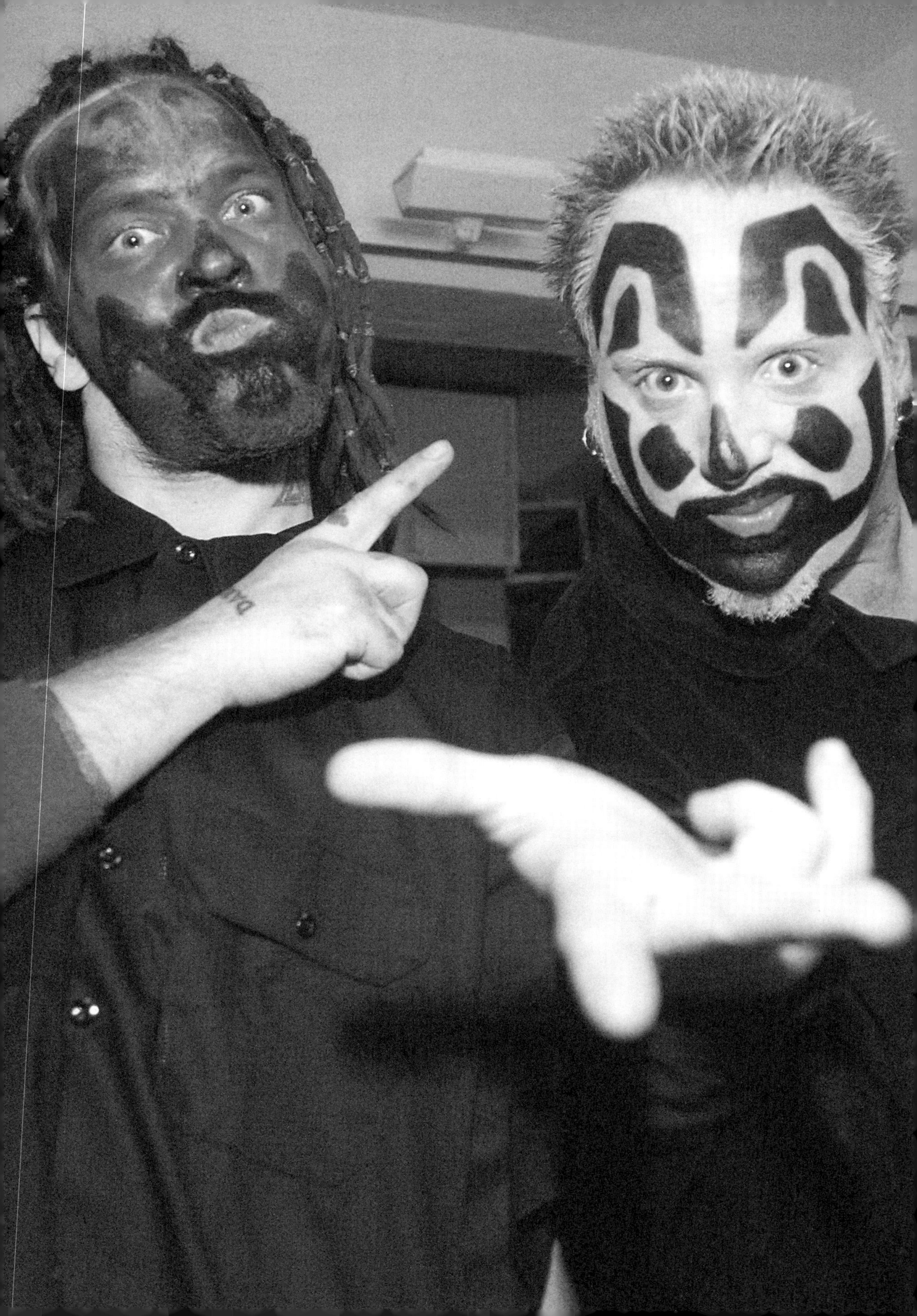

The Bomb

That Spring, during an appearance at the Asylum In-Store tour, a promo tour for *The Amazing Jeckel Brothers*, Insane Clown Posse were signing autographs and CDs when Alex stopped the line. The last time Alex interrupted the boys at an in-store signing, it was with the bombshell that Disney pulled *The Great Milenko* from the shelves. This time the news was much better: They'd been offered $100,000 to play Woodstock '99. For ICP, the invitation was a semblance of recognition from the mainstream music industry that had eluded them so for so long.

The duo played an hour-long set in the early evening on Friday, July 23. "When it came time to perform," Violent J., recalls in *Behind the Paint*, "we found out that Korn was going on halfway through our set on the other stage. Frankly, I thought nobody was going to be there to see us, because of that, and plus we were actually playing on what I considered to be the scrub stage." J.'s fears were unfounded; they had thousands of enthusiastic crowds waiting to see them. Their set included versions of "Chicken Huntin'," "Boogie Woogie Wu," "Down Wit the Clown," and "F**k the World," as well as other songs and skits. It might have been Woodstock, but their set was pure Insane Clown Posse at their most outrageous. In addition to paying Psychopatic crew members in clown make up to streak across the stage, according to Violent J., their show had more "mad naked bitches" on their stage than any other act. Faygo, of course, was everywhere.

The band's only complaint was that the typical intimacy of their shows was impossible because of the size of the stage and the crowds. Regardless, the festival provided a lot of exposure for the band.

The boys invited rap-metal acts Biohazard and Coal Chamber to join them on a twenty-three-date U.S. summer tour to support *The Amazing Jeckel Brothers*. Originally slated to appear on the tour, rapper Kool Keith pulled out because of pressure from fans. Apparently they didn't share the clown love.

Nevertheless, expectations for the tour were high. In a June 15 interview with MTV News, Coal Chamber vocalist B. Dez Fafara shared his enthusiasm for the mix of bands. "I think it's unexpected," said Fafara. "We've never toured with the Clowns, and we heard they were nuts, and we need that kind of thing surrounding us; otherwise, it gets boring."

Unfortunately, Coal Chamber wasn't a good fit for the tour. In addition personality conflicts between the two bands, according to ICP, Coal Chamber wasn't drawing enough fans in to warrant the amount they were getting paid per show. Coal Chamber played only two shows on the tour. Publicly, both bands cited "production problems" as the reason for the split.

In true ICP style, the split turned into a media spectacle. Coal Chamber enumerated their complaints about their treatment on the tour to MTV News days after they were bumped. The next day, New York City shock-jock Howard Stern hosted Violent J. and Shaggy on his morning show (ICP were fans and frequent visitors to the controversial show). Coal Chamber's Michael "Bugs" Cox and Meegs Rascon came into Stern's studio while he was on live with Violent J. and Shaggy. Interestingly, the four band members were able to talk amicably about the split. The problems began when a rep from Coal Chamber's record label, Roadrunner Records, joined the discussion.

Things got more interesting the following day when Violent J. and Shaggy returned to the show for a rehash with Coal Chamber's manager—none other than Sharon Osbourne, wife of Ozzy, reality TV star, and ICP's equal in people skills. A thirty-minute exchange of insults ensued. At one point in the fracas, Osbourne threatened a lawsuit. Violent J. responded by inviting Osbourne to "buff my pickle." Coal Chamber's camp filed the lawsuit that September.

An article in the August 20 issue of *Rolling Stone* recounted Stern's response, "You guys oughta tour with this lawsuit," Stern said. "It's fantastic."

Thankfully, ICP's relationships with summer tour mates Biohazard, Coal Chamber replacement Mindless Self Indulgence, Krayzie Bone, and Psychopathic Record mates Twiztid remained positive.

With Island/Def Jam's support for the band on the wane, it was once again up to ICP to ensure the success of their latest album. The boys toured to support *The Amazing Jeckel Brothers* through spring 2000. It was a busy time for the Psychopathic Records crew. In addition to producing new albums by Kottonmouth Kings and Twiztid, planning for a three-day festival for ICP fans was well underway.

Everyone got a huge scare early in the Millenium. On January 10, during a show at the House of Blues in Chicago, Shaggy fainted and fell off the stage into the crowd. According to an MTV News report filed several days later, when paramedics reached him, he was unconscious and had stopped breathing. They were able to revive him on site, but he was taken to Northern Hospital for treatment and observation. A combination of the flu and abnormally low blood sugar caused his collapse. ICP was forced to postpone several shows, but Shaggy was up and running again after a brief rest at home.

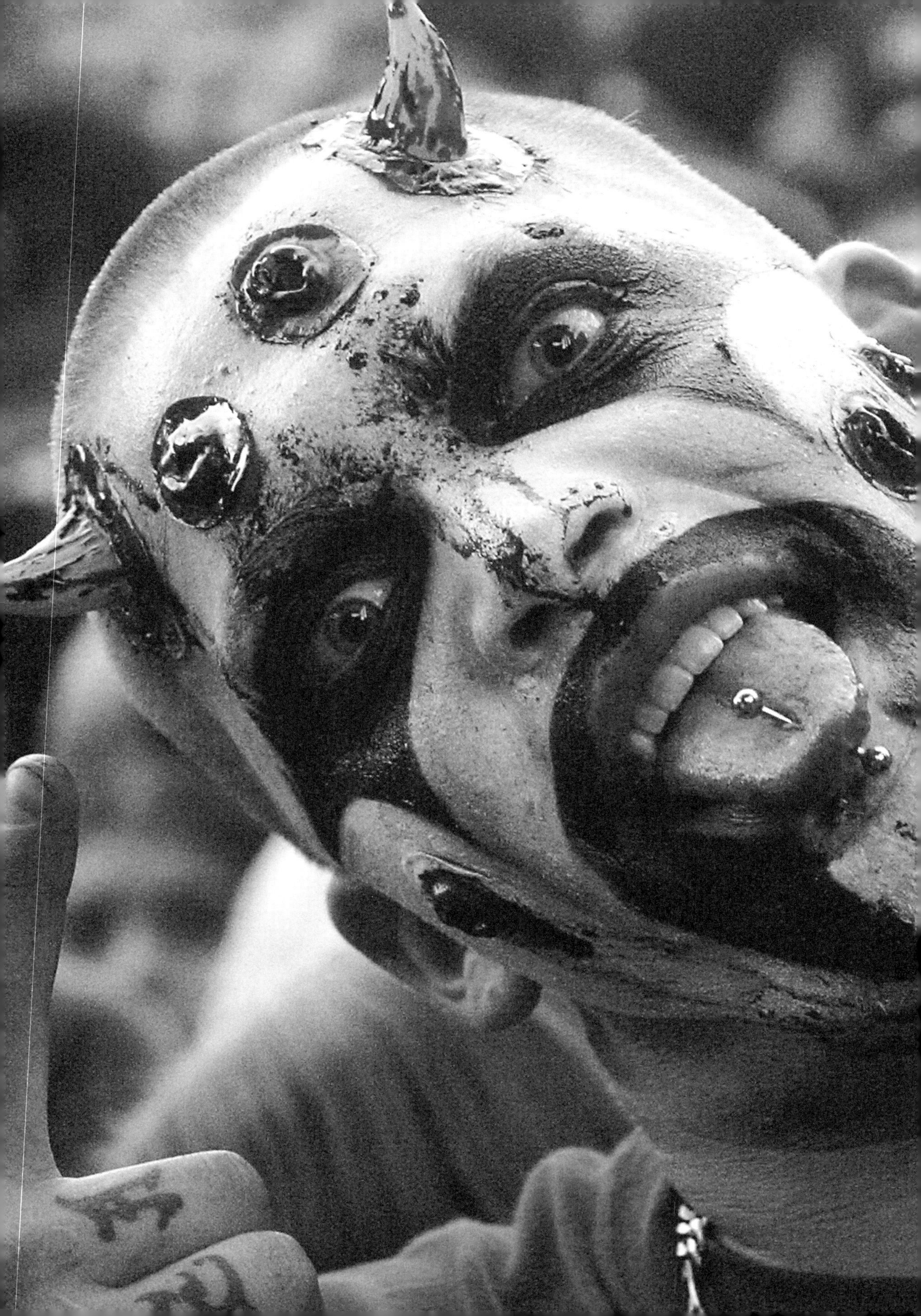

Juggalo Nation

Throughout their career, Insane Clown Posse rarely got props from the press, radio, or MTV. It could have been a lonely road to nowhere, but because of the loyal support of their fans, the band was able to continue to do what it loved: Make music. Very early on ICP recognized that their fans were important, and from the beginning they made it a point to make sure the Juggalos knew that they appreciated that support. Far beyond sharing their Faygo with the crowd, Violent J. and Shaggy were serious about entertaining their fans. From creepy crime scenes to alien invasions, their sets were always elaborate and always changing. More than performing songs, their shows were about the theatrics, the interaction of the fans with the band, and the interaction of the fans with each other.

An annual event since its inauguration in July of 2000, the Gathering of the Juggalos combines all the elements of a single Insane Clown Posse show, blows them up, and stretches them out over several days. A gathering is a Woodstock for Juggalos—only with more to do and more fun. In addition to shows by ICP and guest artists, the first Juggalo gathering, held at the Novi Expo Center in Novi, Michigan, featured an exhibition of ICP concert sets; Juggalo Championshit Wrestling matches; seminars; a haunted house; the premeire of Big Money Hustlas); contests, including a "Sleep with Shaggy" contest and a Miss Juggalette contest; and myriad games.

For the 7,000 fans who attended the three-day festival, it was apparently well worth the $60 ticket. Mark Thompson, who was interviewed after the show by MTV news correspondent Adam Graham, received the trip to the Gathering for his high-school graduation present traveled from New York

The Story of I.C.P.

State. "It was so fresh," Thompson said. "You couldn't ask for much more. I would drive twenty-four hours to get to the one next year."

For ICP and the Psychopathic Records crew, the Gathering was the culmination of years of hard work. Fans weren't the only ones who had enjoyed the Juggalo weekend. In *Behind the Paint* Violent J. says that after many months on the road, he and Shaggy really became re-energized from the experience.

"It was a non-stop f**kin' Juggalo world, together for one weekend," Violent J. recalls. "It was like Ultra Man making it back to the sun for a few days, for Joey and I. It was so new and exciting, and the fact that it all went off so smooth just made it THE FAT DOSE of karma we needed. It was incredible for three days straight."

Juggalo Nation

After the triumphant experience of the inaugural Gathering of the Juggalos, it was time for Violent J. and Shaggy to focus on creating new music. The sixth and final Joker's Card was looming on the horizon, but Violent J. wasn't ready to record it yet. Inspiration from the Dark Carnival had yet to materialize. Instead, he and Shaggy began work on a collection that they would release as two separate but related albums: *Bizzar* and *Bizzar*. The first half was recorded in Detroit with Mike Clark producing. As the album progressed, however, tensions started to grow between Clark and the band. For a change of scenery, J. and Shaggy finished work on the new tracks in Denver, Colorado.

When they returned to Detroit, they decided it was time to open their own recording studio. Alex hired local indie musician and studio designer Mike Puwal to put the studio, which ICP had already dubbed, The Lotus Pod, together. Mike would soon become part of the Psychopathic family.

Bizzar and *Bizzar* hit stores on Halloween. Despite the long months of touring the previous year and the success of the Juggalo Gathering in July, the albums only reached #20 and #21, respectively, on the charts. Because they'd produced two albums, Island paid to produce two videos for the releases "Tilt-A-Whirl" and "Let's Go All the Way," a cover of pop singer Sly Fox's release from the 1980s. "Let's Go All the Way" was getting good radio play—it's one of the few songs that's not crude or explicit. MTV actually accepted the video, it was getting regular airplay, albeit very late at night.

ICP made a clever attempt to get the video out in front of more people. Every fan Web site put up a call for Juggalos to request "Let's Go All the Way" for Total Request Live. For weeks, fans e-mailed and called the request line, but MTV continued to show the video only late at night.

ICP honed their tactics, coordinating fans to send their requests to TRL all on one day. Several hundred Juggalos from Connecticut, New Jersey, and New York converged under the TRL window (they'd be on camera during the live broadcast) at MTV headquarters in Times Square in support of the video. But just as the show was going to air, Viacom security guards and New York City police herded ICP fans out of the camera sightlines. MTV later informed ICP's label that programming executives pre-screen bands for TRL eligibility.

So much for MTV's warm embrace. It was time for Insane Clown Posse to get crackin'. With few breaks in between a multiple-leg tour ICP, toured the country with Marz (a rap-metal band whose lineup included three ex-Ministry members). The tour went relatively smoothly, but it wouldn't be the Posse without a little drama: In March, promoters attempted to cancel a concert after a bomb threat was called in to the police. According to MTV News, the lights went up during Marz's set, and the audience was told the show was cancelled due to technical difficulties. A confrontation erupted between angry fans and local police. Marz frontman Zlatko Hukic claimed police exacerbated the situation by targeting the front row of the audience with pepper spray in order force them to leave the venue.

The Story of I.C.P.

And on June 14, in Columbia, Missouri, local police arrested Violent J. on an outstanding warrant. According to MTV News, the warrant stemmed from an incident in which Violent J. allegedly attacked employees of a St. Louis radio station after one of the disc jockeys insulted him on air. "There were police cars everywhere," J. told MTV reporter Joe D'Angelo. "like they were arresting Charles Manson. I've been arrested my fair share of times, and I've never seen this many police cars arrest anybody." Perhaps they were Eminem fans.

Insane Clown Posse hosted the Gathering of the Juggalos 2001 in mid-July, this time at the Seagate Center in Toledo, Ohio. Peaceful for the most part, fans got a bit out of hand when they rushed the stage on the last night of the festival, forcing ICP to leave just halfway through their set. The angry crowd tore apart the stage set and destroyed equipment. According to MTV reporter Brian Hiatt, fans had "breached Juggalo etiquette" by not waiting until the final song of the evening to tear down the stage. Before the chaotic ending, however, the second annual Gathering once again featured Psychopathic label bands, as well as Vanilla Ice and Marz. In addition to Juggalo Championshit Wrestling, attractions included a Juggalo-Juggalette marriage ceremony, a skate park, and water cannons filled with Faygo.

The Fall of 2001 was eventful for the band. Island/Def Jam chose not to renew their contract, a move the band had anticipated since the 1999 consolidation of the two labels. All of their subsequent albums would be released on Psychopathic Records. At the end of September, ICP launched the Hatchet Rising Tour in support of Tales From the Lotus Pod, which they recorded as a collective with label mates Twiztid and Blaze Ya Dead Homie. And not to be content unless they were juggling many projects simultaneously, Violent J. and Shaggy were hard at work developing The Juggalo Show, for XM Satellite Radio.

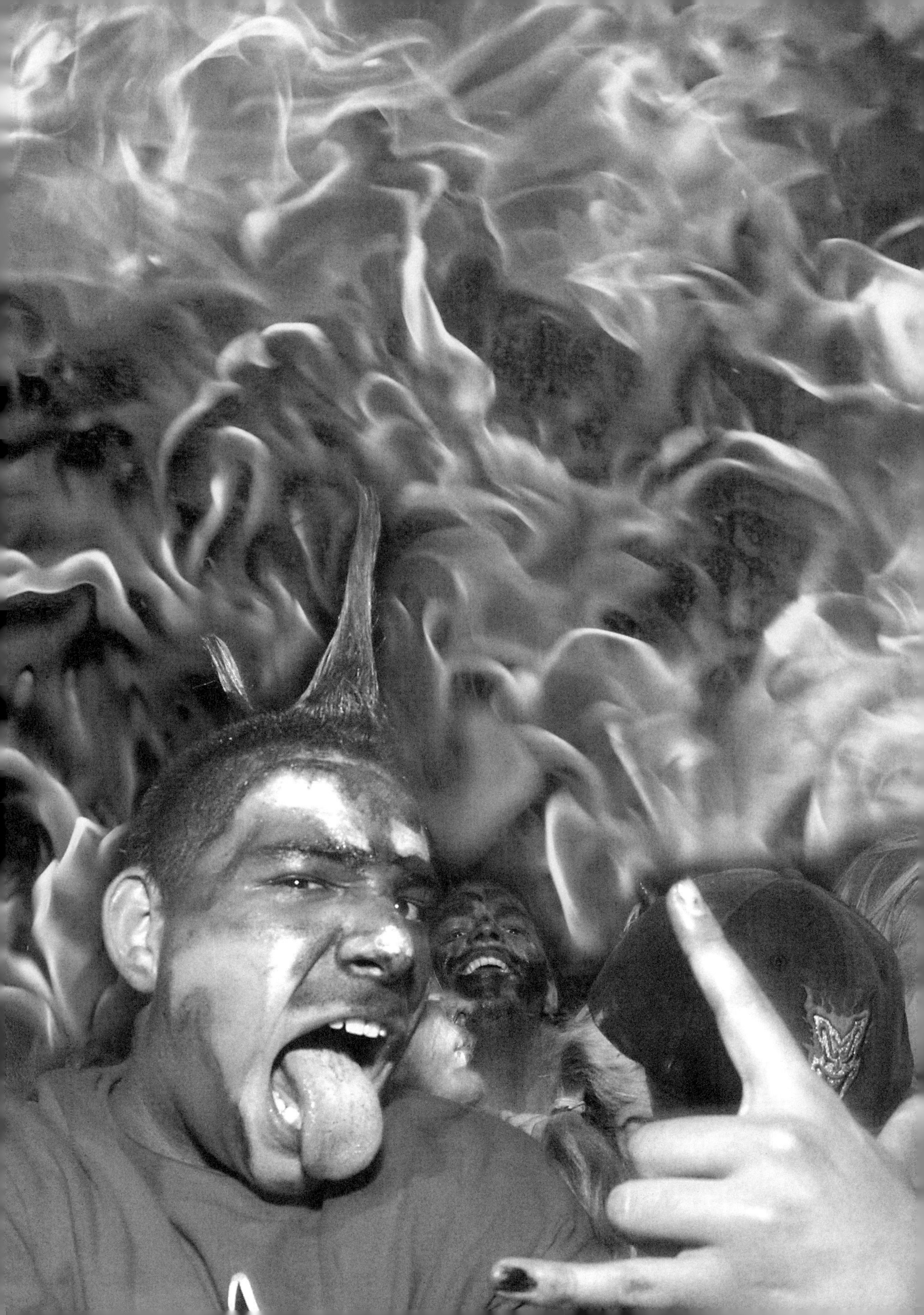

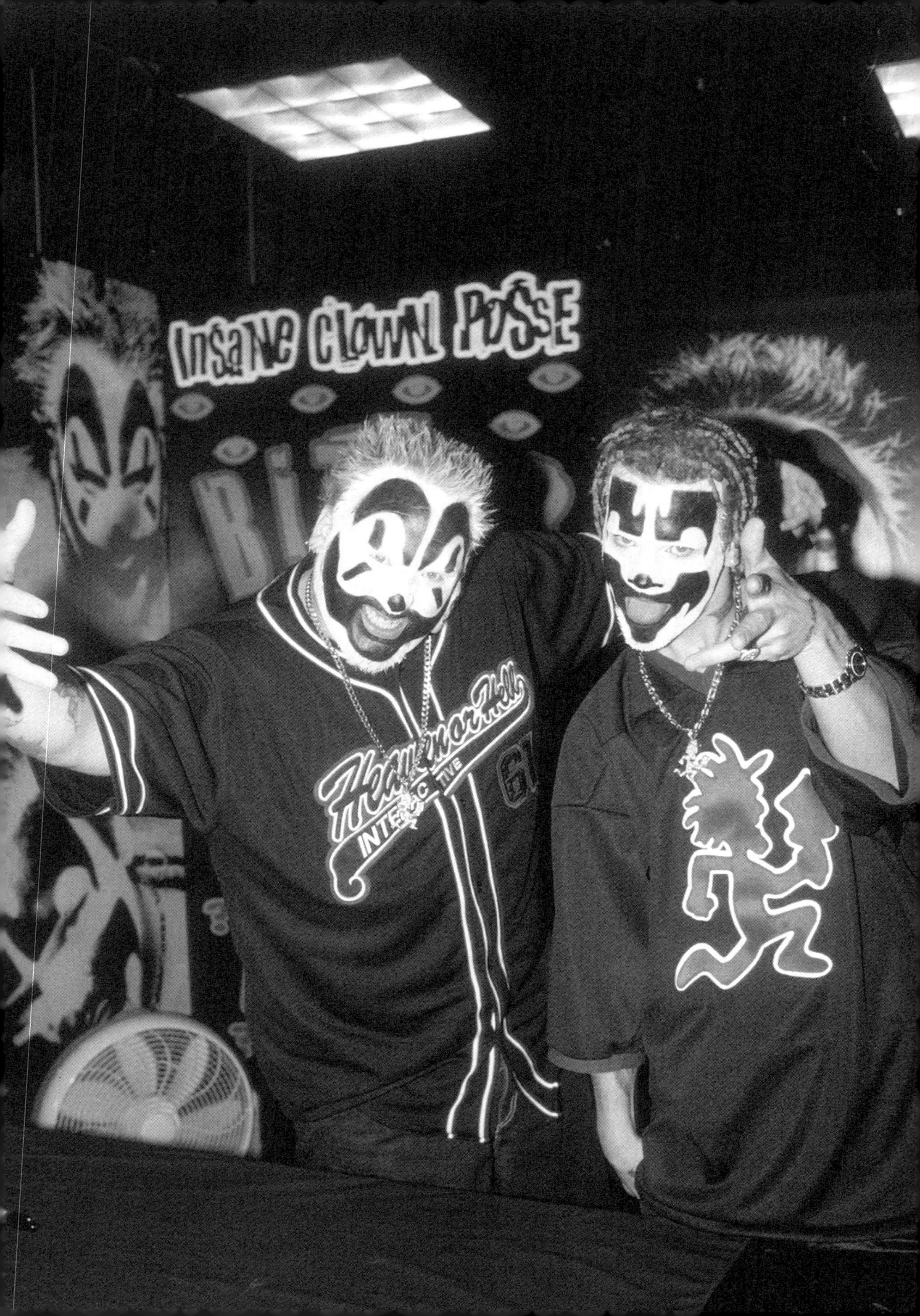
INSANE CLOWN POSSE

Thy Unveiling

After years of constant touring and maintaining a high profile, Insane Clown Posse dropped from public view at the end of 2001. The Dark Carnival was once again making itself felt, and in order to channel the message of the sixth and final Joker's Card, Violent J. and Shaggy needed time to focus. Violent J. recalls this period away from the world as vital, not just to the development of the message of the album, but also as a time to reflect on his life to that point.

Ultimately, the sixth Joker's Card would be released as two separate albums. The first, *The Wraith: Shangri-La* revealed the last message the Dark Carnival would convey. The new character they introduce is the Wraith, which according to ICP, "is a presence that is synonymous with thy crumbling of time itself...He walks upon worlds forgotten, and descends from Heavens; fade into gray to witness thy death of all mortal things, so that he may guide thy departed upon thy path that they have chosen."

In other words, the Wraith is the Grim Reaper, and when you die, he'll lead you down the path you've chosen by the summation of your actions in life. Throughout the album the clowns reveal that their songs with their grisly, psychotic, sexually explicit, misogynistic, and often downright silly lyrics are essentially modern-day fairy tales set to a beat. Fairy tales, like ICP songs, are often grisly, violent, and creepy, but their purpose is demonstrate to the reader that there are consequences to their actions. In the seventeenth and final track, "Thy Unveiling", Violent J. and Shaggy spell it out:

"Who invented Juggalos and Juggalette and f**kin Faygo showers? / What about that feeling you get when bumping our shit, who's behind these Juggalo powers? /

This ain't no f**kin fan club, It aint about making a buck / Don`t buy our f**kin action figures bitch, I dont give a f**k / It ain't About Violent J or Shaggy, the Butterfly or seventeen. / When we speak of Shangri-La, what you think we mean? / Truth is we follow GOD, we've always been behind him, / The Dark Carnival is GOD and may all Juggalos find him!"

Insane Clown Posse explains their purpose and philosophy in this track, as well as in "Crossing the Bridge," and "It Rains Diamonds," but as with all of the Joker's Cards, not every song is serious. In "Thy Staleness," the clowns mock themselves, and there are several songs that are just shout outs to the fans including "Juggalo Homies," and "We Belong."

With the release of *The Wraith: Shrangri-La* in November 2002, came a change in attitude for the clowns. After years of hard work, they understood their message and they understood the success they'd achieved. In an October 2002 interview with MTV news reporter Joe D'Angelo, Violent J. sums up how he was feeling at the time: "Not only did we find light at the end of the tunnel, but we found naked chicks, the finest Faygo products...everything!"

Life was raining diamonds. No doubt helped by years of anticipation, *Shangri-La* debuted at #15 on the charts. As they stepped out to support the new album in the U.S. and throughout the world, their new outlook took on a subtle but definite outward manifestation: Instead of black-and-white greasepaint, their make up now included color.

Of course, you can't know what heaven is unless you have something to compare it to. Nearly two years after ICP unveiled *The Wraith: Shangri-La*, they released the promised second half of their sixth Joker's card: *The Wraith: Hell's Pit* on August 31, 2004. *Hell's Pit* marks the end of the Joker's Card saga. After the positivity of the Shangi-La era, this was a return to the truly dark "Wicked Shit" that ICP were known for. Whereas *Shangri-La* is about redemption, the goal of *Hell's Pit* is to remind the listener that if they don't embrace righteousness, hell is not a pretty place to end up.

"Into the Darkness," "Every Day I Die," and "Burning Up," feature unrelenting imagery of pain and regret. In "Burning Up," ICP points out the difference between prison and Hell:

"And ain't no guards playing cards ain't no uniforms needed / you the only one around, butt-naked bloody and bleedin' / With seven demons in your ear, got you believin' you're a heathen, talk you into pulling out your own intestines to get even / You were born with the shine, but you lost it down the line, you f**ked life up and you can't rewind."

"Suicide Hotline" provides a humorous break, albeit it a dark one. Violent J.'s character has an exchange with a hotline worker; his girlfriend breaks into the conversation, and he reminds her to "bring the blunts."

With tour mates Mack 10, Mushroomhead, and ABK, the clowns went on the road to support the album in October and November 2004. On November 7, fans got out of hand prior to a show at the Albuquerque Convention Center in New Mexico. According to an article on *Pollstar.com*, fans were trying to get into the facility before the doors were open. Local police pulled forty disruptive would-be attendees from the crowd.

"People that started screaming, swearing and rock throwing—basically inciting a riot—went to jail," officer Gene Campbell told local station KOB-TV. Once the concert started, however, the crowd calmed down. Nevertheless, ICP has been banned from returning to the venue.

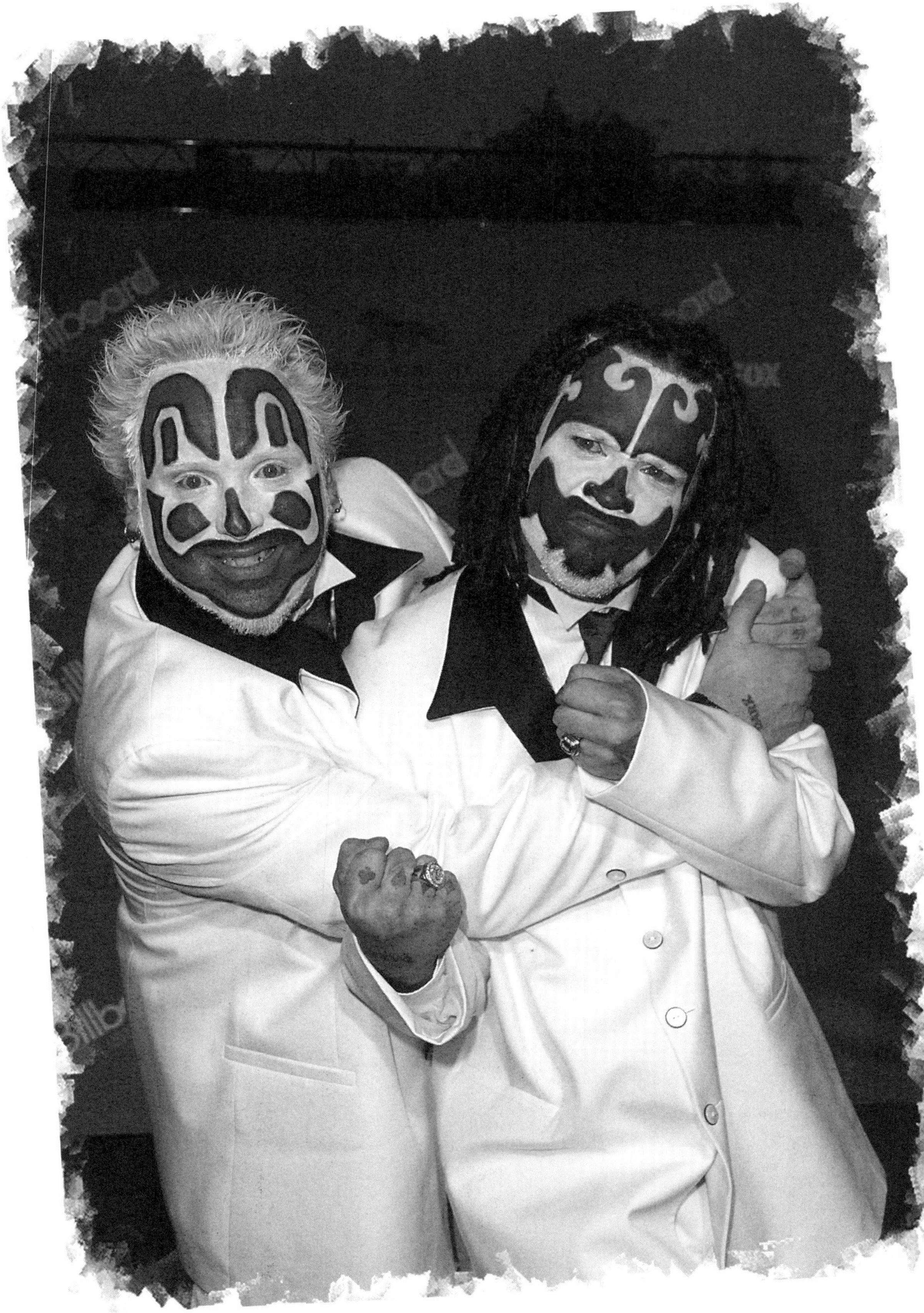

Like It Like That

As of printing, Insane Clown Posse has been recording together for fourteen years. For a band that's often called the most reviled, that would be impressive enough. But along the way, they launched a successful record label with friends and family, managed to pick up five Gold and two Platinum records, started their own wrestling federation, and most importantly, have built an extremely loyal fan base that populates their concerts and festivals and buys their merchandise. "Maybe I'm getting old, but everything is just the bomb," Violent J. said in a 2002 interview with MTV news, "It's raining nothing but diamonds all over my face."

They're getting older, but Violent J. and Shaggy don't seem ready to slow down any time soon. On May 17, 2005, the duo released their newest EP, *The Calm*. They've got their annual Gathering of the Juggalos just around the corner. Beyond that, who knows what these impresarios of the unexpected will do next?

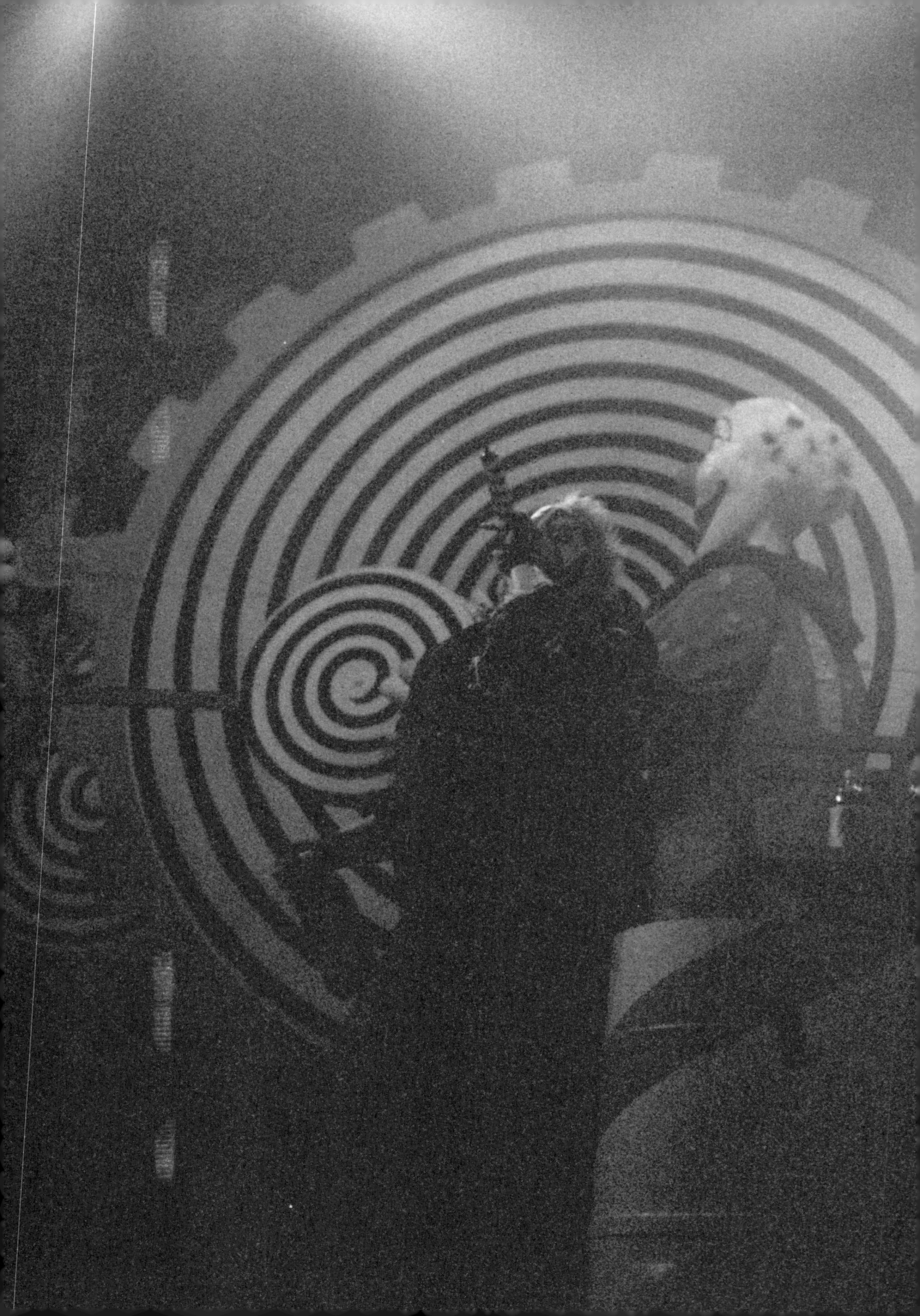

Discography

EPs

Dog Beats (Inner City Posse)
Ghetto Zone / Wizard of the Hood / Life at Risk / Dog Beats
Psychopathic Records, 1991

Beverly Kills 50187
Beverly Kills / 17 Dead / The Stalker / In the Haughhh! / Chop! Chop! / Joke Ya Mind
Psychopathic Records, 1993

The Terror Wheel
The Dead Body Man / Skitsofrantic / The Smog / Out / I Stuck Her with my Wang / Amy's in the Attic
Psychopathic Records, 1994

Carnival Christmas
Santa's a Fat Bitch / Red Christmas / Santa Killas / It's Coming
Psychopathic Records, 1994

Tunnel of Love
Intro / Cotton Candy / Super Balls / Ninja / Stomp / Prom Queen / My Kind of Bitch / When I Get Out / Mental Warp
Psychopathic Records, 1996

Full Length

Carnival of Carnage
Intro / Carnival of Carnage / The Juggla / First Day Out / Red Neck Hoe / Wizard of the Hood / Guts on the Ceiling / Is That You? (w/ Kid Rock) / Night of the Axe / Psychopathic / Blackin' your Eyes / Never Had It Made / Your Rebel Flag / Ghetto Freak Show / Taste (w/ Esham)
Psychopathic Records, 1992

Ringmaster
Wax Museum / Murder Go Round / Chicken Huntin' / Mr. Johnson's Head / Southwest Song / Get Off Me, Dog! / Who Asked You / The Dead One / My Fun House / For the Maggots / Wagon Wagon / The Loons / Love Song / Bugz on my Nugz / House of Mirrors (w/ Capitol E) / Ringmaster's Word
Psychopathic Records, 1994

Riddlebox
Riddle Box / The Show Must Go On / Chicken Huntin' (Slaughter House Mix) / Toy Box / Cemetery Girl / 3 Rings / Headless Boogie / The Joker's Wild / Dead Body Man / Lil' Somthin' Somthin' / Ol' Evil Eye / 12 / The Killing Fields / I'm Coming Home
Jive Records, 1995

Full Length continued...

The Great Milenko
Intro (w/ Alice Cooper) / Great Milenko / Hokus Pokus / Piggy Pie / How Many Times? / Southwest Voodoo / Halls of Illusion (w/ Slash) / Under the Moon / What is a Juggalo / House of Horrors / Boogie Woogie Wu / The Neden Game / Hellalujah / Down with the Clown / Just Like That / Pass Me By
Island Def Jam, 1997

(Disney's Hollywood Records released a censored version earlier in the year. In addition to forcing ICP to record toned down versions of many of the songs, they pulled "Under the Moon," "Boogie Woogie Wu," and "The Neden Game." After buying the band out of its ill-fated contract with Hollywood, Island Def Jam rereleased the original version produced by the band.)

Mutilation Mix
Request #1 / Cemetary Girl / Clown Luv / Wagon Wagon / Request #2 / Psychopathic / Southwest Strangla / Never Had It Made / Chicken Huntin' - Slaughterhouse Mix / I Stuck Her with my Wang / The Neck Cutta / Red Neck Hoe / Request #3 / I'm Comin' Home / Super Balls / The Stalker / Wizard of the Hood / Skitsofrantic / 3 Rings / Request #4 / Murder Go' Round / Request #5 / Southwest Song / F**k Off! / The Dead Body Man / Cotton Candy / Dead / Request #6 / The Neden Game / House of Wonders + Mike Clark Bitchin'
Island Def Jam, 1997

Forgotten Freshness 1 & 2
Forgotten Freshness Vol. 1
Hey Vato / Dead Pumpkins / Fat Sweaty Betty / Willy Bubba / Graveyard (w/Project Born) / F**k Off! / I didn't Mean to Kill 'em / Southwest Strangla / Santa's a Fat Bitch / Witching Hour (w/Myzery)
Forgotten Freshness Vol. 2
Mr. Johnson's Head Remix / Clown Love / Hokus Pokus Headhunta'z Remix / Red Christmas / House of Wonders / Mr. Rotten Treats / Piggy Pie (Old School) / I'm Not Alone / 85 Bucks an Hour (w/Twiztid) / Halloween on Military Street / Dog Beats / Mental Warp
Island Def Jam, 1998

The Amazing Jeckel Brothers
Intro / Jake Jeckel / Bring It On / I Want My Shit / Bitches (w/Ol' Dirty Bastard) / Terrible / I Stab People / Another Love Song / Everybody Rize / Play with Me / Jack Jeckel / F**k the World / The Shaggy Show (w/Snoop Dogg) / Mad Professor / Assassins / Echo Side (w/Twiztid) / Nothing's Left
Island Def Jam, 1999

Bizzar
Intro / Bizzar / Cherry Pie (I Need a Freak) / Questions / Mr. Happy / Radio Stars / My Axe / If / Let's Go All the Way / Let a Killa / Juggalo Paradise / Crystal Ball
Island Def Jam, 2000

Bizaar
Intro / Take Me Away / Fearless / Rainbows & Stuff / Whut / Still Stabbin' / Tilt-a-Whirl / We Gives No F**k / Please Don't Hate Me / Behind the Paint / My Homie Baby Momma / The Pendulum's Promise
Island Def Jam, 2000

Forgotten Freshness Volume 3
Intro / Cartoon Nightmares / Posse on Vernor / Fly Away / It / Run! / Nuttin' But a Bitch Thang / Just Another Crazy Click / Take It! / Super Star / Every Halloween / The Mom Song / Insane Killers / Confessions / When Vampiro Gets High / Take Me Home
Island Def Jam, 2001

The Wraith: Shangri-La
Walk into thy Light / Welcome to thy Show / Get Ya Wicked On / Murder Rap / Birthday Bitches / Blaaam!!! / It Rains Diamonds / Thy Staleness / Hell's Forecast / Juggalo Homies (w/Twiztid) / Ain't Yo Bidness / We Belong / Cotton Candy & / Popsicles (w/Zug Izland) / Crossing thy Bridge / Thy Raven's Mirror / Thy Wraith / Thy Unveiling
Psychopathic Records, 2002

Hell's Pit
Intro / Walk into the Darkness / Suicide Hotline / C.P.K.'s / Truly Alone / Everyday I Die / The Night of the 44 / The Witch / Bowling Balls / 24 / Burning Up / Sedatives / In my Room / Basehead Attack / Angels Falling / Manic Depressive / Real Underground Baby
Psychopathic Records, 2004

The Calm
Intro / Rollin' Over / Rosemary / Crop Circles / We'll Be Alright / Like It Like That / Off the Track / Deadbeat Moms (featuring Esham)
Psychopathic Records, 2005